A STRUGGLE

For disabled people and people with learning difficulties the transition from school to college, work or training can be stressful and frustrating. Job choices are often restricted, and they face barriers which are beyond their control. This book is about their struggle for choice, setting special needs in further education in a socio-political context.

The book focuses on the notion of 'transition to adulthood' for students with special educational needs, exploring it in terms of class, race, gender and disability differences and relating it to social, economic and political influences. The book analyses employment opportunities, education and training choices and possible degrees of community participation, addressing the problems encountered by both students and those staff who support them. Its distinctive approach recognises discrimination and challenges stereotyping.

The book is intended to confront complacency, encourage dialogue and debate and suggest ways forward in what the authors perceive is a difficult struggle for choice. Each chapter includes a set of questions which can be used as the basis for discussion.

Jenny Corbett is Senior Lecturer in Special Education at the University of East London. She has varied teaching experience, including secondary and special schools, and further and higher education. She also works as a consultant, and on research and staff development committees for Skill: The National Bureau for Students with Disabilities. **Len Barton**, currently Professor of Education at the University of Sheffield teaching on the M.Ed/MA programmes, has been both a student and a lecturer in FE. He is the founder and editor of the international journal, *Disability, Handicap and Society*.

A STRUGGLE FOR CHOICE

Students with special needs in transition to adulthood

Jenny Corbett and Len Barton

London and New York

First published 1992
by Routledge
11 New Fetter Lane, London EC4P 4EE

Simultaneously published in the USA and Canada
by Routledge
a division of Routledge, Chapman and Hall, Inc.
29 West 35th Street, New York, NY 10001

Typeset in Palatino by Michael Mepham, Frome, Somerset
Printed and bound in Great Britain by
Mackays of Chatham PLC, Chatham, Kent

British Library Cataloguing in Publication Data
A catalogue record for this book is available from the British
Library.

Library of Congress Cataloging in Publication Data
Corbett, Jenny, 1947–
    A struggle for choice : students with special needs
in transition to adulthood / Jenny Corbett and Len Barton.
    p. cm.
Includes bibliographical references and index.
ISBN 0–415–08000–2. – ISBN 0–415–08001–0 (pbk.)
1. Handicapped youth—Education—Great Britain.
2. Handicapped youth—Vocational education—Great
Britain. 3. Handicapped youth—Employment—Great
Britain. Adult education—Great Britain.
I. Barton, Len. II. Title.
LC4036.G7C67   1992
371.91—dc20   92–9324
                                               CIP

To Elizabeth and Richard

CONTENTS

ACKNOWLEDGEMENT

We would like to express our appreciation to Carolyn Hallahan and Roz Hill, current lecturers working with students with special needs, for giving us valuable feedback on the manuscript.

INTRODUCTION

Major changes are currently taking place in further education and training initiatives. These will have far-reaching implications for policy and practice in the beginning of the twenty-first century. However, the extent to which they reflect a coherent vision of future provision is debatable. For example, the Government White Paper, *Education and Training for the 21st Century*, (DES 1991a) has received a very mixed reception. In his 'Platform' article in the *TES*, which Brenchley (1991) entitled 'Muddling to the Millennium', he states:

> When the need was for a consistent funding policy, raising the combined contributions from the whole training sector to a level approaching even half that of our major competitors, we get a piece of short-term pragmatism and a very convenient scapegoat.
>
> (Brenchley, 1991, p. 16)

In a series of thoughtful criticisms, Brenchley argues that political values have shaped the recommendations within this Government White Paper. This political stance includes a prioritising in which adult education has been neglected. A recent editorial comment in the *TES* (5 July 1991) reflected that adult education, which it recognised as a vital issue in relation to equal opportunities, had been given scant attention. This was despite the Education Minister, Tim Eggar, noting that the role of adult education, as an opportunity for widening access, could not be underestimated. The inherent contradictions embodied in these developments reflect the combinations of politically competing objectives and muddled thinking.

1

An awareness of both this political context and confusion leads Maclure (1991) to suggest that

> What must now be created is a robust, clearly-understood, *system* of education and training, backed by efficient, clear-sighted, open and strong but flexible institutions, which will provide a sturdy framework within which the needs of all 14–18 year-olds can be met.
> The ultimate object must be a system which can carry large numbers forward without question and without agonising – a system which everyone takes for granted as part of the natural order of things.
>
> (Maclure, 1991, pp. 22–3)

So comprehensive a system would encompass the needs of young and old, offer a diverse choice of opportunities and include people with disabilities and learning difficulties. The current threat to adult education is particularly damaging for those students who wish to pursue non-vocational courses. Those with learning difficulties and disabilities can be seen to be clearly vulnerable in this respect. One of the key criticisms of current changes is that specific areas remain as afterthoughts. This results in the aforementioned groups remaining mainly invisible. Their interests, choices and rights are often neglected. They are the subject of this book. The degree and intensity of their difficulties has led us to the title – 'A Struggle for Choice'.

EXPLORING OUR PERSPECTIVES

We approach this area, both of us having worked with young people and adults who have disabilities and learning difficulties. Our experience in further and adult education has made us aware of the complexities involved and the frustrations of supporting students without an effective power base. In addition to attempting to keep abreast of contemporary literature, three factors have informed our understanding. These involve the insights derived from teaching lecturers in further and adult education and exploring the issues that concern them; the supervision of research-based higher degree work in which these practitioners investigate professional aspects of their practice;

and finally, our own research projects which keep us close to current developments in a changing field.

We have written this book because we feel that there is a need for literature which seeks to place the issues relating to special educational needs within a socio-political context. Whilst there continues to be a strong body of literature which critically evaluates pre-vocational education and training generally (e.g. Ainley, 1990; Gleeson, 1990; Hollands, 1990) this tends to pay only peripheral attention to young people with disabilities and learning difficulties. That body of literature which does address their needs tends to focus specifically upon curriculum, assessment, teaching approaches and policy, without extensive articulation of socio-political perspectives. We feel that a combination of crucial elements from both these important sources will provide fertile ground for examining contentious issues.

In our commitment to this task, we are aware that we may be subjected to criticism for taking a negative stance. By raising contentious issues, we could be accused of overlooking individual needs and failing to acknowledge the considerable developments since the early 1980s. Our argument is that the time is now right for reflective criticism. Provision for students with special needs in further and adult education and training is now well established and documented (e.g. Bradley, 1985; Dee, 1988; Cooper, 1989; Sutcliffe, 1990). These students are now included and supported by the Education Act 1988. Most colleges of further education have special needs co-ordinators in post. A wide range of courses for these students has developed nationally (Stowell, 1987). Special needs is now on the agenda in colleges as part of an equal opportunities policy. If this whole-college approach is to make any lasting impact, it has to be within a socio-political perspective. Far from taking a negative approach to these issues, what we hope to encourage is an informed and constructive dialogue in which difficulties are confronted. There is much talk of 'empowerment' and 'entitlement' in relation to students with special needs. Where this is centred upon individualised models of development, it avoids problematising complex issues. Moreover, such a focus highlights personal inadequacies rather than challenging social inequities. We feel that the way forward is to place special needs in a broader context. This is not a destructive process. Rather, we see it as a release from a restrictive focus into an arena which offers possibilities for change.

In order to problematise certain preconceptions, we want to stimulate the kind of discussion which recognises that there are no easy answers. This is not a comfortable activity. Nor should it ever be assumed otherwise. The struggle for real, participatory democracy inevitably involves challenging the status quo.

By focusing on a range of contributory factors, including class, race and gender, there are certain aspects we will not address. These include detailed case study examples of curricular practice, staff development and individual student progress. We feel that these areas are already well covered by authors such as Faraday and Harris (1989) and that a different perspective can compliment these other approaches.

Furthermore, we are not presenting a skills-based sequence of 'tips for teachers'. Neither do we offer the definitive statement on any of the issues we examine. We are still struggling with them ourselves. Not only do we invite our readers to be reflective about their own practices but also we try to be critical in evaluating our own approach. In providing three questions for discussion at the end of each chapter, we hope both to raise controversial issues and to allow for criticism of our perspectives. We anticipate that this book will have a wide readership, including both students and lecturers. We hope it will be informative and relevant, providing discussion of current initiatives and recent literature drawing from, for example, those varied sources already highlighted. As the writing of this book has been a truly collaborative exercise, we hope that the finished product will contribute to the development of collaborative learning in action.

We have been involved in a series of arguments and counter-arguments in the process of writing this book. Many of the struggles we have engaged in have been disturbing and, in some instances, the outcomes have yet to be resolved. However, the process has resulted in a greater self-awareness, including a recognition of our limitations and doubts. We have also learnt to listen to one another's perspective. This involves sharing insights, raising questions and learning to respect our mutual contributions.

The central issues which this book seeks to engage with are extremely complex. The work context in which practitioners operate has become increasingly stressful and demanding. We recognise the serious implications of both these factors and do not underestimate the difficulties involved. Rather than negate our commitment to collaborative work, they provide the impetus for it. Supporting one another within this taxing process has been a valuable strength. We would hope that the material we offer does, in some small way, enable the force of support networks to be realised.

TAKING A STAND

We start from a recognition of the discrimination that disabled people and those with learning difficulties face. This discrimination is deep-rooted, pervading all aspects of their lives. For many of them, it brings experience of poverty, unemployment and a marginalised status.

Focusing on education and training opportunities alone, we feel, creates an artificial distinction. Much of the literature on students with special needs in further education concentrates upon developing an appropriate curriculum (e.g. Dee, 1988; Faraday and Harris, 1989). This approach is too restrictive for our purposes. For us, it underplays the impact of structural inequalities. This is only part of a wider system of unequal power relations. It is against this context that we believe questions relating to these vulnerable groups should be addressed. Our bias, as authors, is to take the side of these oppressed groups. Their alienation and frustration requires further understanding. We feel angry on their behalf. In our critical examination of the inadequacies in recent developments, we are seeking to challenge the status quo which has promoted discrimination.

Political action by disabled people and those with learning difficulties has significantly increased. This is a necessary part of the struggle for change and a real force for empowerment. Such movements face complex and difficult decisions. In a discussion of the progress of the disability movement, Oliver (1990), the well-known disabled activist, succinctly identifies current dilemmas:

Should it settle for incorporation into state activities with the prospect of piecemeal gains in social policy and legis-

5

lation with the risks that representations to political institutions will be ignored or manipulated? Or should it remain separate from the state and concentrate on consciousness-raising activities leading to long-term change in policy and practice and the empowerment of disabled people, with the attendant risks that the movement may be marginalised or isolated?

(Oliver, 1990, p. 128)

In making this statement, Oliver illustrates the contradictory nature of empowerment within an oppressive social context. This reinforces our contention that we are grappling with complex questions to which there are no easy answers. What we hope this book will offer is a series of perspectives and ideas which can stimulate further debate and dialogue. The questions we raise are part of our commitment to encourage critical inquiry.

1

SETTING THE SCENE

Education is high on the government's agenda. This interest has been encouraged through issues such as falling standards, ill-discipline, restricted choice and a call for increased effectiveness in schools and colleges. One of the perceived outcomes of these deficiencies in the education system is the effects on the nation's ability to be competitive in the international market place. Thus the control of education, including post-school experience, involving its management and the nature of the outputs are central topics of concern for the government. The emphasis of a market mentality is clearly evident in a process of change in which the role of the consumer is paramount. Relationships between education and the needs of industry have become additional factors in shaping the organisation, content and governing bodies of institutions.

Concern has been expressed over the extent of government interference in the content of the curriculum, the composition of the National Curriculum Council (NCC) panels and the lack of consultation at different stages in the accelerated process of change. The ultimate reservation is powerfully articulated in a National Union of Teachers' (NUT) document which maintains that

> It is clear to the teaching profession and others that the timetable for implementing the National Curriculum prioritises political goals rather than educational ones.
>
> (NUT, 1990a, p. 15)

Teachers are both the agents of change and the subjects of criticism. Growing evidence suggests that the past decade of extensive innovations and demands is having its impact on the morale and personal well-being of the teaching body. To implement these new initiatives requires sustained enthusiasm, commitment and confidence. However, increasing numbers of teachers acknowledge feelings of disillusion and exhaustion. A contributory factor is the tensions between, on the one hand, lack of appropriate financial and professional support and, on the other hand, reservations they have regarding the nature and ultimate benefit of some of these changes.

THE NATURE OF FURTHER EDUCATION

For the purpose of this book, we are focusing upon further education in England and Wales, as Scotland has a separate system of provision. The way in which further education colleges are distinctive from other education systems such as adult education and secondary education is complex and is described in the Appendix, specifically for readers who are unfamiliar with the British educational context.

Colleges of further education were designed to be local resources, open to change and providing relevant vocational training. Thus, colleges in Hull and Plymouth developed courses in Nautical Studies; colleges in Nottinghamshire, Mining Studies; colleges in Central London, a wide range of specialist areas like Fashion and Furniture. Although the Education Act 1944 indicated that the role of further education was to offer both educational and recreational provision, the more traditional technical institutes tended to concentrate on the former rather than the latter. A preservation of advanced work could ignore minority interests in the local community. Recent expansion of community colleges has focused upon offering ease of access, pastoral support and flexibility to meet a wide range of needs.

However, there have been many notable national, as well as local, influences on further education. These include the changes in skills training in relation to the collapse of apprenticeships, which has created a need for staff retraining. Another influence has been a move to control what has been perceived as a confused system. A feature of the education system generally, over the past decade, has been an intensification of competitiveness and accountability. Where the diverse nature of further education has enabled it, in the past, to be left to its own devices:

> Now that it is recognised as being high-cost and competing for scarce resources, both human and financial, it is coming under greater scrutiny.
>
> (Kedney, 1988, p. 30)

An important aspect of this increased scrutiny is governmental response to vocational training in Britain. The New Training Initiative (NTI), established by the Manpower Service Commission (MSC) in 1981, aimed to provide major changes in national systems of training and education. An impetus for change was Britain's appalling record as producing 'one of the least trained work forces in the industrial world' (FEU, 1989b, p. 1). Thus the Youth Training Scheme (YTS) was established in April 1982 to hopefully remedy this. Subsequently, two-year YTS was introduced in April 1986, in order to extend the training experience. Government designs to create a consistent national framework for vocational qualifications resulted in the establishment of the National Council for Vocational Qualifications (NCVQ) in October 1986. This included agreed national standards of occupational competence.

Government attempts to improve the quality and effectiveness of training programmes, validated by national qualifications, need to be set against the recognition that

> Less than half of the 16-plus generation attend school or college after they cease being legally required to do so; only one third of the 17-plus group and less than one fifth of those aged 18 or over choose education or training rather than work without associated further education or the dole.
>
> (Cunningham, 1990, p. 10)

Ostensibly, the government has established and promoted these initiatives and offered a public discourse of commitment. Within this process, teachers who were initially sceptical and reluctant to involve themselves in such programmes have come to see some value in them. Change in teaching styles and learning outcomes has improved the level of teacher support. However,

9

more recent events have begun to demonstrate the shallowness of government commitment. A dramatic cut in funding for both the Technical and Vocational Education Initiative (TVEI) and Youth Training (YT) has jeopardised the effectiveness of such innovations. The seriousness of this can be seen in that:

> Education directors and councillors talk of betrayal by a government which encouraged them to undertake elaborate preparations and then halved the promised funding at the last minute. Teacher associations condemned the irresponsibility of the cut.
>
> (Jackson, 1990, p. 10)

An Opposition survey indicated that ten training centres for disadvantaged young people were closed because of the Government funding cuts, 1,400 youth training places cut from other schemes and some 200 trainers made redundant. This led Derek Fatchett, Labour's spokesman for education and employment, to say:

> The Government seems content to allow these young people to drift into the low-paid low-skill twilight zone of the labour market, or even worse, into abject poverty and homelessness.
>
> (Dean, 1990, p. 6)

It would be misleading to assume that such decision are the result of a lack of resources. Rather it is a reflection of the divisive nature of government policy in that disproportionate sums of money have been allocated, for example, to city technology colleges and increasingly to grant maintained schools. Thus priorities are with supporting institutions which legitimise the market as the sole determiner of quality and provision. Questions of social justice and equity become marginalised in this context.

CRITICAL PERSPECTIVES ON THE NEW VOCATIONALISM

Criticisms of Government policy in 14–19 education and training initiatives are now long established. They broadly include

the following areas: the cultural dominance of the New Vocationalism; the threat to a comprehensive ideology; scepticism
created by changes in the status and format of Youth Training;
the inequality of regional disparities; discrimination towards
minority groups; the uneven quality of training; the patronising
nature of a social skills curriculum and the minimal level of
actual training required in a service-sector economy.

Its most vociferous critics, however, acknowledge the value
of the new vocationalism in supporting local policy initiatives
which often produce imaginative results and in addressing the
curricular needs of those school leavers for whom school was
previously an irrelevance (Ainley, 1990; Gleeson, 1990a). Yet,
alongside these potential advantages, they perceive a clear in-
crease in government and employer intervention in educational
issues and an apparent narrowing of choice. Coles (1988) refers
to the 'cultural dominance' of the Manpower Services Commission (MSC) and it successors, through which financial
control is not the only or most pervasive agent of oppression:

> The heart of 'the new vocationalism' is centred, not just on
> financial control and incentives, but in the very language,
> thinking and culture which has been so successfully
> spread by the MSC.
>
> (Coles, 1988, p. 8)

This language has now even permeated HMI (Her Majesty's
Inspectorate) documents on work-based further education
(DES, 1990) in which 'Commercial realism' and 'Business enterprise' are selected as integral facets of training. Plunkett (1987)
perceives this cultural shift as a marked threat to traditional
educational values and suggests that teachers can reverse this
ideological dissolution, whilst Dickinson and Erben (1989)
imply that some aspects of progressive education have actively
fostered the growth and establishment of this new culture, by
rejecting traditional cultural values as elitism.

Arising from this debate is a concern about the threat to a
comprehensive ideology. The culture of 'the new vocationalism'
is not a culture for all, for

> It represents a 'vocationalization' of working class school-
> ing and involves a shift from a policy of fully

comprehensive education to that of 'socially appropriate' training.

(Brown, 1988, p. 132)

The New Training Initiative has never become a comprehensive form of education and training for all 14–19 year olds but, rather, remained a provision for unemployed school leavers (Ainley and Corney, 1990, p. 140). This has created an uncomfortable fragmentation of 14–19 provision which 'takes us ever further away from the concept of a broad, integrated and open system of post-compulsory education and training' (Green, 1990, p. 18).

The confused and contradictory nature of post-compulsory education and training has led to inferences that Britain appears unable to decide which route to take and to accusations of barely masked governmental hypocrisy. Constant changes and regular modifications in Youth Training programmes suggest muddled and ineffective policy-making, in which

Training providers no longer have to follow the old YTS design framework but are 'free to adapt patterns and mixes of training and methods of trainee assessment best suited to the . . . particular circumstances'.

(Ainley, 1990, p. 41)

These circumstances will differ markedly in relation to regional and socio-economic contexts.

Whilst only about a quarter of 16 year olds nationally enter Youth Training, in parts of the North this will involve the majority. This disparity highlights the contrast between those schemes in affluent areas which are likely to lead to secure employment and those in regions of socio-economic deprivation which become mainly preoccupied with 'managing unemployment whilst inculcating a work ethic necessary for the acceptance of the dead end jobs on offer to the majority of trainees' (McKie, 1990, p. 19). Part of this required 'work ethic' includes a passivity and compliance promoted in 'social and life skills' (SLS) training, an aspect of the hidden curriculum which has gained prominence in the new vocationalism.

Discriminatory practices towards minority groups in training programmes has included gender stereotyping of occupational roles and the relegation of black youths to schemes at one remove from employment. Young women selecting untraditional options in YT can become pioneers who risk peer group ridicule (Beloff, 1986). When, despite an equal opportunities rhetoric, the Training Agency has perpetuated traditional gender roles in YT, Cockburn (1987) suggests that young women need to make 'a definite refusal' (p. 11). She recognises the stress of this move against prevailing conformity:

> There is scope within the Youth Training Scheme for supporting young people in the needed refusal. Many YTS workers are putting courage and imagination into the task. Yet the political and economic context of YTS render it, in spite of their best intentions, a vast machine mass-producing the age-old inequalities.
>
> (Cockburn, 1987, p. 12)

Black young people face difficulties in finding employment (Fenton and Burton, 1987) and are also often perceived as having 'special needs' in training programmes (Cross and Smith, 1987). There are now Development Officers who promote equal opportunities (Ghua, 1988). Yet, there can be contradictions within apparently innovative schemes. In a YT workshop containing a high proportion of black trainees and seeking to combat traditional prejudices from employers, there was evidence of covert racism among staff (Corbett, 1990b). The impact of racist and sexist practices from fellow trainees can create more damage and inhibit the process of change (Hollands, 1990).

Cockburn (1987) refers to this emphasis upon social skills as 'a patronising slur on young people's personal qualities' (p. 24). It is a curriculum that is behaviourist in its emphasis, focusing upon modifying perceived individual deficiencies rather than upon the development of a critical awareness of social inequities. Gleeson (1990b) suggests that

> despite the apparent veneer of social relevance in SLA there is little reference to the individual learning about society, or of the student acquiring knowledge and concepts which take him/her beyond the immediate and the parochial.
>
> (Gleeson, 1990b, p. 193)

This restricted and narrow definition of social roles is replicated in what many perceive as the limitations of a 'competence' approach. The rhetoric of the new vocationalism has introduced the concept of 'occupational competence', in which skills have to be seen to be mastered and tasks broken into their component parts. In a technological society in which the only expanding area is the service sector, it is generally low level skills which are being required of 16 year old school leavers (Finegold and Soskice, 1990). An emphasis upon task analysis

> devalues those particular human skills of intuition and creativity that are irreplaceable by machinery and so often necessary to cope with the uncertainties of unprecedented change. They are being lost in favour of purely mechanical, repetitive and quantifiable certainty.
>
> (Ainley, 1988, p. 132)

An image of 'quantifiable certainty' might be taken to typify that purposeful language of oppression featured so prominently within this debate. Such an emphasis reiterates the cultural dominance of 'realism' and 'enterprise' which characterises the ideology of the new vocationalism.

Perhaps the development which can be seen to exemplify this pursuit of 'quantifiable certainty' is the prominence given to the recently established Training and Enterprise Councils (TECs). The DES (1991a) White Paper is unequivocal about their intention to

> give Training and Enterprise Councils more scope to promote employer influence in education, and mutual support between employers and education.
>
> (DES, 1991, p. 3)

The implications of so narrowly defined a purpose of education are significant. It seems ironic that such a focused emphasis in further education emerges alongside a commitment to 'breadth and balance' in the National Curriculum, exposing just one of many contradictory features in current government legislation.

SPECIAL NEEDS IN FURTHER EDUCATION AND TRAINING

By the term 'special needs' we mean those young people whose disabilities or difficulties in learning have led in their schooling to the provision of some form of specialised assistance in the form of aids or adaptations, welfare support or a modified curriculum. Thus, they enter further education or training with a past history which influences their capacity to benefit from new opportunities. If they have come from segregated special schools in which they might have been overprotected, a large college can be overwhelming. If their experience of secondary schooling is one of prolonged failure, they may have correspondingly low expectations of progress in further education.

The period between 1980 and 1990 has seen the rapid expansion of provision in further education for students with special needs, as courses throughout the country have proliferated (Stowell, 1987). However, this growth has been erratic and uneven regionally, some areas having developed provision long before others (Bradley and Hegarty, 1981). This has led to some students with disabilities, particularly those in wheelchairs, being forced to attend colleges some distance from their homes and even to participate in classes not of their choosing just because these are the only places and courses which are accessible.

The integration of students with special needs into colleges of further education has been gradual, reflecting changing attitudes and the impact of an equal opportunities rhetoric (Corbett, 1990a). There have always been some students with special needs in further education but these have tended to be those whose physical disabilities did not prevent their full participation in mainstream curricula. When students with learning difficulties were first introduced, they were carefully selected to ensure that they would be seen to benefit from further education and training (Newton and Robinson, 1982). In the 1990s, an emphasis upon 'entitlement' has brought a wide range of students into colleges, including those whose learning difficulties are perceived as severe and those adults in day centres whose exposure to educational activities might have ended years before.

Under the terms of the Education Reform Act 1988, curriculum entitlement is seen as an

> obligation on providers (or those co-ordinating provision) rather than learners, and as a right to participate in certain learning experiences in addition to working towards particular outcomes.
>
> (FEU, 1989a, p. 1)

The NUT (1990b) reflects upon the potential impact of the Education Act 1988 on future provision for post–16 students with special needs by suggesting that

> The 1988 Education Act appears to plug the loophole in the 1944 Education Act by making it the duty of every LEA to 'secure . . . adequate facilities in FE colleges' and to 'have regard to the requirements of persons over compulsory school age who have learning difficulties'. However, in conferring power to LEAs to 'do anything which appears . . . necessary' for students with special educational needs, the 1988 Act allows local authorities to retain the element of choice as to the extent to which they use those powers. Nevertheless, the 1988 Act has allowed, for example, Sutton LEA in co-operation with its Social Services Department, to assess the special educational needs of its post–16 students and give them statements of provision in its FE colleges. Such statements, where the right courses are not available, may define specific programmes of provision for the individual student. Sutton has also decided to allow the full assessment and statement process to continue up until the age of 30.
>
> (NUT, 1990b, pp. 2–3)

As the focus on 'specific programmes' implies, a modified and separate curriculum has developed in further education as a response to the perceived rigidity and inappropriateness of traditional vocational and academic provision.

This curriculum has evolved in stages. In 1985, the staff development package supported by the DES, *From Coping to Confidence* (Bradley, 1985), presented a teaching framework designed for students with moderate learning difficulties, who were then coming into FE and training schemes in increasing numbers. In 1986, a curriculum framework was published which had been developed in response to the evident needs of students with complex physical and additional disabilities, attending the accessible workshop at North Nottinghamshire College (Hutchinson and Tennyson, 1986). By 1988, as students with severe learning difficulties were entering FE from both schools and training centres there was the dissemination of *New Directions* (Dee, 1988) which offered a series of teaching approaches and curricular options built around the issues of normalisation, self-advocacy and entitlement. In keeping with new national initiatives, a 1989 staff development pack, *Learning Support* (Faraday and Harris, 1989), focuses upon negotiated individual learning in which integration is viewed as a whole-college responsibility.

Whilst these initiatives were attempts to provide curricular substance to what had been an ad hoc and often grossly inadequate provision, they served to support what had become established as a separate and distinctive area of work in further education. An HMI Report (DES, 1989) recognised that 'few curriculum statements include any reference to progression into FE or training, although some mention employment as an ultimate aim' (p. 18). This separation of curricular ideology means that 'it is not easy to relate the aims and objectives of most special needs courses to other college provision to which students might aspire' (DES, 1989, p. 18). This effectively recreates a special educational system within further education mirroring that which exists in compulsory schooling.

Gradually, special needs departments have grown and more staff become involved. However, this has not significantly altered the low status which has characterised this area. Many staff working with students with special needs are on the lowest levels in the college hierarchy and are, therefore, in no position to enter the bargaining for resources so vital to departmental strength in FE. It is only where special needs co-ordinators have management status within a college that they can make an equal opportunities policy become anything more than rhetoric. The DES document *A 'Special' Professionalism* (DES, 1987) outlines a range of staff development programmes, designed to ease the full integration of students with special needs, yet the implementation of such training depends upon the level of commitment of governing bodies for whom this may be a low priority.

Within these special curricula created in FE, an emphasis upon social and life skills has dominated many programmes. This might be justified in relation to the need for appropriate behaviours to be taught in order to foster normalisation or it might be seen as a way of socially integrating unacceptable young people. Until very recently, when such an intrusion has been challenged, such programmes were accepted as part of what constituted a preparation for adult life for disadvantaged students.

In Youth Training and Employment Training programmes, trainees with special needs are often placed in workshop-based provision rather than with employers. This places them at an immediate distance from potential employment and often subjects them to a poor quality of training which compounds their minority status (Rosie, 1988; Corbett, 1990b). In such schemes, the emphasis is upon developing deferential attitudes and punctual, reliable attendance rather than upon acquiring skills. Recent changes in YT policy indicate that trainees with 'special training needs' will be

> identified by the Careers Service, which will then place them in one of three categories: A, requiring Initial Training for up to six months; B, those who will not realistically achieve a level 2 National Vocational Qualification; C, those who will achieve such a National Vocational Qualification only with additional help. However, it is not clear how the quality of the TECs' special training needs provision in YT will be monitored and evaluated (if at all).
>
> (Ainley, 1990, p. 39)

Such reflections imply that the governmental muddle over the new vocationalism is extended into training in the 'special needs' area. Despite the common threads which link criticism of the new vocationalism generally with evident contradictions in provision for students with special needs, there has been comparatively little challenge to either the special curriculum or to the inequalities within social skills programmes and training schemes designed for this group. Perhaps this has arisen for several reasons. There is, firstly, the issue of emotional rhetoric attached to any debate on providing for 'the disabled' or for people with 'learning difficulties'. It is almost as if sentiment clouds critical judgement when the notion of disability is involved, such that what would become areas of concern in other contexts are often overlooked. The powerful tradition that professionals involved with special needs are caring, patient and loving, make it difficult to raise questions, for example, about low-expectations or patronising and over-protective practices. Secondly, a focus on responding to individual needs avoids serious confrontation with broader social issues. By giving a privileged status to individualistic explanations the question of special needs tends to be viewed as a personal trouble and not a public issue (Mills, 1970). Thirdly, staff in this field have been marginalised and, therefore, rarely play a central political role in their institutions. This encourages a depoliticised image of special needs in FE. Fourthly, the increasing vocationalism and skill-based emphasis of FE and special needs programmes tends to engender technical or *how* rather than *why* questions. The latter are viewed as politically biased, irrelevant or not in the best interests of the people involved. Finally, with the introduction of a powerful market mentality, issues of cost effectiveness, inputs and outputs, generate expectations for immediacy of returns. Short-term interests minimise the complex and fundamental nature of the difficulties. Rapid expansion of provision has often outstripped the careful development of whole-college policies. This has resulted in special needs rarely being addressed as part of a more general equal opportunities policy (DES, 1989). Where practitioners themselves feel marginalised, this makes for defensiveness in the light of criticism.

A SOCIO-POLITICAL APPROACH

Education takes place in a political context and is itself political. It involves the allocation of resources and the setting of priorities. Values get translated into sets of policy statements and the most powerful are those whose values are significant in the formulation and implementation of policy. (Marshall *et al.*, 1989). Issues are complex and contentious with people viewing the same topic in very different and conflicting ways. Education has thus been likened unto a battlefield of warring parties with the struggle between unequal groups taking place over objectives, values and meanings (Evetts, 1973; Fulcher, 1989). Questions of social justice, opportunity and quality of experience are significant issues in this process. Concerns over power, influence and control become even more important when they relate to vulnerable groups.

It is absolutely necessary, therefore, that the question of special needs is set within a more general framework committed to equal opportunities. It is necessary because this enables us to identify and declare that there are features of the existing society, policies and practices that are unacceptable, offensive and need to be challenged and changed. Also, importantly, that any attempts to redirect resources to provide opportunities for the most marginalised, disadvantaged and discriminated-against people in society cannot pretend to be apolitical. It also identifies the crucial task of establishing connections between other discriminated-againt groups in order that attempts can be made to engage in common struggles.

However, there are difficulties in taking this position in that equal opportunities is overwhelmingly regarded as being about issues relating to gender and race. Paternalism and the exclusion of disabled people from participation in decision making, is still largely the norm and as Leach (1989) has recently argued in a discussion concerning disabled people and the implementation of local authorities' equal opportunities policies:

> The invisibility of disability as an issue is also the case with many local authority equal opportunity initiatives, where issues concerning disabled people have either been ignored, tacked on to initiatives centrally concerned with race or gender or segregated in low status disability units.
>
> (Leach, 1989, p. 68)

Thus there is no room for complacency.

From our perspective, learning is fundamentally a social activity. Therefore, we must examine the ways in which social contexts contribute to the creation of difficulties for the learner. Needs are not to be viewed as existing in some absolute sense (Dessent, 1987). How they are constructed, perceived, maintained and changed in given contexts become topics of crucial concern. A different set of values and priorities are required which will enable structural issues to be addressed. For example,

20

how can we create institutions which do not exclude people no matter the degree to which they are atypical (Dyson, 1990)?

The approach we are advocating, and through which we address the issues raised in this book, has the following features:

1 It is based on a belief that the manner in which a society deals with minority/disadvantaged groups provides some crucial insights into the nature of that society.
2 It locates the problems as not being within individuals but as arising from the discriminating practices and organisations of society.
3 It places the concern for integration within the wider perspective of human rights, social justice and equality of opportunity.
4 It advocates the importance of relational thinking and views critical analysis as an essential precondition for change.
5 It clarifies the nature of the opposition and the extent of the struggle involved if the changes demanded are to be realised.
6 It provides an antidote to the pursuit of slick, easy and short-term solutions, for what are complex and fundamental issues.

CONCLUSION

Our commitment to this approach is motivated by our understanding of the serious, extensive, social and economic inequalities and relations which characterise our society. Piecemeal, surface reforms are inadequate. These profound iniquities of the system will need to be challenged if the oppressive and unadaptive features of our society are to be changed. It is these that disabled people increasingly see as the issues to be tackled (Abberley, 1987; Oliver, 1990). Nor is it sufficient merely to argue for attitudinal change. Attitudes are not free floating. They are expressed from within given sets of social relations, which are themselves structured by economic and cultural factors. Institutions embody these and legitimise them through their organisation, ethos and practices. The issues to be addressed therefore entail political, ideological and structural factors. These are complex and contentious, extending to the use of language. We have chosen, for example, to use the term 'disabled people' instead of 'people with disabilities'. This is because we agree with Oliver (1990) that disability is both a political and cultural issue. Where 'disabled' is seen as a positive characteristic, it is overtly used and not placed awkwardly as an appendage. So, we consciously use the term 'disabled people'.

We are alert to attitudes which depict critical analysis as essentially negative. We have a different view of the notion of critical discourse. By identifying those disabilist and offensive features of the world which are the means through which people suffer emotionally, psychologically, physically and materially, critical analysis provides an impetus and means through which change can occur. Without this form of reflection, people's views will remain conservative or doctrinaire (Carr, 1986). Therefore, it is understanding which leads to change that we are interested in. Too much is at stake for anything less than this.

Nor is the issue merely reducible to a question of resources. This underplays the significance of ideology and politics which shape our views of 'normality' and our commitment of material support. It is also these powerful factors, according to Fulcher (1989), that have influenced a form of 'special needs' discourse resulting in the exclusion, and thus marginalisation, of vulnerable groups of people.

A crucial issue relating to this form of discourse is the significance given to key concepts like 'adulthood'. In the next chapter we will examine the extent to which prevailing notions of 'adulthood' individualise and simplify complex issues, presenting an undifferentiated view of young people and the social world in which they live.

QUESTIONS FOR DISCUSSION

1 Is it necessary to set the issue of special needs within an equal opportunities framework?
2 To what extent do you share the view of society which the authors represent in this chapter?
3 We would feel unable to discuss post–16 educational provision adequately in anything other than a political context. What is your perspective on this stance?

2

ADULTHOOD

One of the essential principles informing our analysis is a recognition of the complex and contradictory nature of the social world. Our everyday language tends to belie this. A pragmatic concern to function continuously, in given contexts, limits the degree to which alternatives are considered. This need to work within a simplified structure extends, most vividly, to professionals in the human service field. Wolfensberger (1989) illustrates the disjunction between professional rhetoric and practice when he maintains that

> In the human service field, we are confronted by a great deal of rhetoric, and by an avalanche of documents, that proclaim that services are beneficent, charitable, benign, curative, habilitative, etc. These then are the manifest functions of human service organisations. But while services may be some of these things some of the time, they also commonly perform latent functions very different from those proclaimed ones, including ones that are competency-impairing, destructive of independence, that are actually dependency-making and dependency-keeping, health debilitating, and outright death-accelerating and thus killing.
>
> (Wolfensberger, 1989, p. 26)

Whilst for some readers Wolfensberger's language may seem unacceptably emotive, the use of such imagery highlights the contradictions professionals face. They are not free agents but are constrained by the structures of the organisations in which they work. The impact of these constraints is to legitimise a simplification of complex issues in order to function and display effective control. Professional discourse, therefore, is not to be received uncritically but to be subject to careful analysis.

A key example of a complex issue being reduced to a simplistic perspective is that of the professional discourse surrounding the notion of 'transition to adulthood'. Within this discourse, the characteristic features of adulthood are identified as autonomy, productive activity leading to economic self-sufficiency, social interaction and a valued role within the family (Fish, 1990). Whilst difficulties relating to these characteristics are acknowledged, they are rarely examined within a socio-political framework. It is our intention in this chapter to provide such an analysis.

We need to begin our discussion by defining 'adulthood'. The inference from the above list of characteristic features is that they combine together to form the **state** of adulthood. However, we contend that adulthood is a **process** and not a state. As Griffiths (1989) suggests, most of us experience adulthood as a number of small changes developing over a period of years. Adulthood can also be contradictory in its expression. Few of us adopt the equivalent level of adulthood in every aspect of our lives. Furthermore, it is a process which is experienced differently as a result of such key factors as class, race and gender. Gaining employment is seen as one of the main components of adulthood.

A central strand of our perspective is that society is based upon fundamental inequalities and that these structure people's experiences and opportunities in powerful ways. The problem of, for example, racism is thus serious and one which compounds the oppressiveness of black people's lives. Key institutions are not excluded from this problem. In Nottingham a police officer, Surinder Singh, took his case of racial discrimination to the Industrial Tribunal. In the first case of its kind the outcome raises serious concern, as Duncan Campbell notes,

> After a record of 82 days of hearings and 66 witnesses a picture emerged of the enormous gulf between the perceptions of some of Nottingham's senior CID officers and the young Asian and black officers who wish – or wished – to serve with them.
>
> (Campbell, 1990, p. 23)

24

The tribunal upheld the allegations of PC Singh that he had suffered serious racial abuse from fellow officers and had been treated unfairly with regard to his attempts to work with the Nottingham CID. Such cases across the industrial scene could be multiplied. However, the disturbing feature of this illustration is that disabled black people are, at least, doubly disadvantaged in this socially divisive context. The extent of their disadvantage and abilities to cope with such experiences will also be affected by their socio-economic standing.

Research has illustrated that black young people face difficulties in finding employment (S. Fenton and Burton, 1987) and that young people from the inner-city are more likely to experience unemployment than their non-inner-city counterparts (Gray *et al.*, 1989). Thus the extent to which individuals are able to participate in employment will be an indicator of the reality of their adulthood.

MARGINALISED ADULT STATUS

Inequalities of access into the labour market and the differential rewards involved are forcefully reflected in the experiences of disabled people, as among those who are employed there are typically fewer on high earnings and in good conditions of work and many are working longer hours for lower earnings. For young people with learning difficulties opportunities to obtain unskilled employment are decreasing with technological change. Griffiths (1989) offers an illustration of how recent reductions in unemployment nationally conceal significant differences in both geographical areas and amongst specific groups:

> For example, a laundry which provided 50 jobs may close and instead two estate agents, three specialist retail outlets for electronic goods, a restaurant and a solicitor's office may open in the same area. There will have been no statistical job loss but most of the ex-laundry employees may become unemployed because they cannot be recruited for the new jobs. New arrivals or commuters from another area fill them.
>
> (Griffiths, 1989, p. 12)

In this example, opportunities to gain valued features of adult status are constrained by economic realities. More generally, within the stubbornness of economic and political inequalities some groups are more vulnerable than others.

The consequent marginalisation of people with learning difficulties impoverishes their experiences of adulthood. In this process they transfer the dependency of their schooling to their adult status. The maintenance of a peripheral position arises from the cumulative impact of past socialisation as John (1986) notes:

> The special education system, then, is one of the main channels for disseminating the predominant able-bodied/minded perception of the world and ensuring that disabled school leavers are socially immature and isolated. This isolation results in passive acceptance of social discrimination, lack of skills in facing the tasks of adulthood and ignorance about the main social issues of our time. All this reinforces the 'eternal children' myth and ensures at the same time disabled school leavers lack the skills for overcoming the myth.
>
> (John, 1986, p. 6)

A central feature of the special school system they have left is its focus upon individualised learning programmes. It also remains a major component in their further education. We feel that this emphasis both simplifies complex issues and avoids addressing evident inequalities. Education is political and takes place in a political context. Working with such groups, therefore, requires more than the teaching of 'appropriately adult' skills and attitudes. It necessitates an involvement in the difficult struggle of achieving something greater than what is essentially a spurious form of adulthood.

THE POLITICAL AGENDA

In advocating this level of commitment we do not underestimate the demands of the task. Nevertheless, from our perspective, working with vulnerable groups entails a moral imperative. The issues are fundamental, including those of social justice, choice and empowerment, requiring long- as well as short-term

26

strategies. However, the former are not easily quantifiable. This exacerbates the dilemma of lecturers in further education who have increasing pressure to be accountable. Thus, they are expected to produce detailed reports which measure the progress of individuals. Such an approach necessitates the adoption of a simplified structure and correspondingly narrowed vision. This forced pragmaticism gives significance to an essentially depoliticised view of the task.

An individualised model avoids acknowledging the political context in which change has to occur. Developing skills and attitudes in the individual is not, of itself, sufficient for removing the inequalities to which we have referred.

Compounding the difficulties staff face is often their own low status within the institutions in which they work. Being relatively powerless themselves, they are in a weak position to empower their students. Engaging in the micro-politics of institutional life will thus be both demanding and complex, necessitating astute political awareness and effective negotiating tactics. However, many staff in this area are unlikely to be confident in such an arena, having come themselves from the restrictive confines of the special education sector. Within this sphere, the focus of attention is on responding to individual needs. Such an approach dominates the professional discourse whilst broader and more critical issues, such as rights, are of less significance. Caring, in this context, is highly individualised. Within FE, caring is about the individual, but the individual within the realities of harsh economic and political conditions. To care in such circumstances unavoidably necessitates political engagement. This involves caring about rights and equity for marginalised, low-status individuals.

DEFINING 'NORMALITY'

The transfer of aspects of the special education sector into FE has introduced a separate and segregated curriculum for students with learning difficulties. In courses entitled, for example, 'Skills for Living', students are trained to adopt characteristics of 'normality' which, it is alleged, are required for their transition to adulthood. This distinguishes them from their peers in FE who are engaged in, for example, vocational training and for whom the status of adulthood is assumed to be implicit.

This central focus on 'normality' illustrates a dichotomy in FE provision in which the tensions between an individualised and societal model are highlighted. The process of 'normalisation' (Wolfensberger, 1975), which relates to being able to integrate successfully into mainstream society, rests responsibility on the individual to adapt and to learn to be more 'normal' than the norm. The essential conservatism of this approach has been modified by Wolfensberger and is now being further questioned, as in this example:

> It is clear from his work that he has a strongly-held view that differences should not be devalued. Yet it is easy to see how people would put a narrow interpretation on his views based on the wording of the principle or a reading of the earlier text. . . . It is apparent that he views society as a unified cultural whole rather than as containing competing groups which are culturally, morally and politically diverse. In assuming that the notion of what is normal is unproblematic, he leaves it to be defined by the dominant group of which the advocate of normalization may well be a member.
>
> (Booth, 1988, p. 105)

When the curriculum calls for the assessment of such displays of 'normality' caring can be seen to be oppressive. As we have already acknowledged, few of us are equally adult in all aspects of our lives. However, because we can present a surface competence in our work roles and social interactions, private inadequacies are not revealed and, thus, not subject to public scrutiny. For disabled people or people with learning difficulties, however, the professional gaze extends into the most intimate aspects of their lives. It is this power to conflate the public and private spheres and make them the legitimate concern of professional judgement which demonstrates the degree of exposure which disabled people have to endure.

In extending the boundaries of normality, professional involvement often encourages vulnerable individuals to become hyper-critical of their perceived inadequacies. In the following example, this student actually exaggerates the deficiencies she anticipates will be evaluated:

one girl's contribution to her Individual Programme Plan (IPP) report illustrates the political pitfall of self-assessment.

My feelings about my IPP Report

I could do an awful lot better in all the areas, especially in the independence area and hobbies area.

I could do better in group discussion and not be so self-centred.

I could also do more to motivate myself.

I could also do a lot more to control my moods.

I would like to prove to everyone especially Audrey and Mum and Dad that I can be trusted and more independent.

(Fenton and Hughes, 1989, p. 144)

Mood changes and self-absorption are common facets of adolescent behaviour. However, a focus on such characteristics is not a component of a traditional curriculum. We maintain that such a curricular focus is oppressive for it forces an unreasonable notion of normality and fosters extreme self-consciousness. Under the guise of empowerment, individuals are exposed to revealing their innermost feelings in a context in which there is a relationship of unequals.

What is normal? In much of the literature the emphasis on training for normalisation is highly selective and evaluates superficial signs of normality (Trower *et al.*, 1978; J. Wilkinson and Canter, 1982). This approach is skill-based and has developed from behavioural training programmes. Within a typical 'Skills for Living' curriculum, independence is equated with the accomplishment of daily living skills like shopping. Yet independence involves more than mere coping with daily living skills. Rather, it entails taking risks, having adventures and experiencing excitement. Yet the following example indicates that disabled people are assumed to experience a different reality:

One Saturday, some months ago, I heard a radio programme about holidays. Amongst the treks to Borneo, and Club 18–30 extravaganzas the presenter referred to a coming item about 'holidays for the disabled'. I listened with bated breath. I love holidays. The item, when it came, described the chance to stay in an institution in another part of the country, to give 'the disabled' a change of scene, and their relatives a breather from them. Now, this is *worthy*; but it is not exciting. No new horizons there. I did not go. But, please remember when next booking for two weeks in Crete, that some people with disabilities will be trundled from one residential home in the Midlands, to another on the South Coast, and be expected to be very, very grateful.

> (Chapman, 1988, p. 18, added emphasis)

Professionals tend to define the reality of vulnerable groups in a restrictive and, thus, unimaginative form (Woods and Shears, 1986). The above illustration is an example of much that characterises the patronage of caring, in which professionals define what is an appropriate experience and recipients are expected to be 'very, very grateful'. Under the rhetoric of compassionate ideals, the asymmetrical relationship of the parties involved is reinforced.

DEVELOPING RELATIONSHIPS

None of us is self-sufficient. We all need to create a balance in which we can express our autonomy, whilst relying upon others for support. However, some of us rely more heavily upon the support of others. People with learning difficulties moving into community homes have been found to be strongly influenced by the quality of their relationship with staff:

> The kind of relationship was therefore a key factor in determining the quality of life of the participant as he or she perceived it. Too often, research pertaining to quality of life has been preoccupied with concrete and easily-measurable variables and has ignored this central, human component.
>
> (Cattermole, *et al.*, 1990, p. 151)

Such a preoccupation characterises for us the professional urge to simplify learning into manageable proportions. Too often this leads to giving a privileged status to observable and assessable skills of a cosmetic nature. An example of a teaching programme which has been highly influential in developing social skills with adults who have learning difficulties is the Copewell Curriculum. The section on Social Interaction typifies, for us, the superficial approach to relationships:

18.3 Spatial behaviour.
Is aware of appropriate distance to maintain when interacting with another individual or individuals.

18.4 Visual contact.
Is aware of acceptable eye contact and makes appropriate use of eye contact in social interactions.

18.5 Bodily contact.
Knows how and when it is appropriate to make bodily contact with others.

(Whelan *et al.*, 1984, p. 96)

These identified objectives remain for us context free, culturally biased and essentially narrowly conservative in their approach. The use of words such as 'acceptable' and 'appropriate' are indicators of the marginalised social status of the group concerned. By presenting a non-problematical view of behaviour, relationships and the social context in which they take place, the important questions are not addressed. We would wish to ask: Who is defining this? In what context? With what purpose? With what consequences for the definer and defined?

A training programme on acceptable behaviours is based on the premise that the conduct of its recipients is by definition inferior. It is also a mechanistic approach which emphasises surface behaviours instead of examining feelings, ideas, attitudes and values (Firth and Rapley, 1990). We would contend that without learning to value oneself, one cannot begin to value others. People with learning difficulties and/or disabilities are constantly being socially devalued. Consequently, assaults upon their self-esteem both inhibit spontaneous expression and make the establishing of relationships with others more difficult. Where the former is displayed it can be interpreted as a justification for the application of a more stringent behavioural programme.

We are all influenced by prevailing concepts of normality. Conventionally, adults who have children wish for a healthy baby. The birth of a child with disabilities is socially regarded as a tragic event. For this woman, however, the birth of her daughter, who was born with the same disability as her, was regarded as 'a real bonus'. She goes on to say:

> She is the perfect baby for me because in learning to completely love her, I am learning to completely love myself. In getting things right for her, I see all the ways in which I had accepted less than the best for myself. How much better than trying to make up for the mistake of existing!
>
> (Mason, 1986)

Such a stance defies much of what constitutes professional judgements. How can a disabled baby be perfect? Mason's delight challenges societal expectations and thus offers a refreshingly alternative perspective. She indicates that this process of learning to value herself, through her daughter, will ultimately benefit both. This example has particular significance for us, as it reveals not only the shallowness of narrowly conservative approaches but also their dangerous limitations. By extending the boundaries of normality and, thereby, questioning the status quo, Mason challenges professional sensibilities. This includes their values, priorities and assessment as to the degree to which people are judged competent and allowed to be involved in the process of key decision-making about their lives.

OPPORTUNITIES FOR DECISION-MAKING

There is an appealing quality to much of the language associated with the notions of empowerment and self-advocacy. The following example captures the liberating spirit of this movement for change:

> There is an increasing demand from people with disabilities themselves that they should be enabled to take a full and active part in all aspects of social life. In particular, disabled people are insisting on their right to services that meet their needs as they themselves define them. Self advocacy is a key aspect of this developing awareness. It emphasises the need for people with disabilities to know

their own rights and, as importantly, for proper attention
to be paid to their experiences, opinions and ideas.

(Clare, 1990, p. 1)

Empowering, within this framework, is directed at the individual. Using the tools of self-advocacy, people with learning difficulties are encouraged to take decisions about their lives, with the support of advocacy groups. We would not wish to underestimate some of the evident benefits and good intentions behind the promotion of empowerment. We particularly welcome the effort to take seriously the experiences and opinions of disabled people. Nevertheless, the perspective we have adopted leads us to raise certain questions:

- To what extent does the promotion of empowerment become a more subtle means of professional control?
- Can a focus on the empowerment of the individual lead to an oppressive outcome?

The issue of adulthood is inextricably linked to the ability to act responsibly. Decision-making is a key act of those who are deemed responsible. It thus assumes a privileged status. Within the rhetoric of empowerment, decision-making is a central component. Yet the realisation of an effective outcome can begin to be accomplished only if existing professional expectations and practices are open to question. In a recent study, for example, which examined the role of day centres for disabled young people, the research indicated that few opportunities for key decision-making were available to those young people despite the operation of ostensibly progressive policies (Barnes, 1990).

Brown and Smith (1989) indicate that a focus on the empowerment of the individual can indeed result in an oppressive outcome if they are to receive services from an overwhelmingly female force of relatives and carers. Poverty and social isolation are key factors in this oppression. It is not empowerment as a concept which is being challenged, but its translation into practice:

Users are saying that they do need services but have a right to be offered them in a way which does not further disempower them and over which they have some control.

Normalisation as an ideology fails to make explicit this
tension between giving value and taking power.
(Brown and Smith, 1989, p. 113)

However, relinquishing professional power is difficult. The
manager of a day centre for adults with learning difficulties
found that staff expectations could actually inhibit empowerment. Several members of the centre were living in a shared
house in which they chose to stay up late watching videos and
not attend the centre regularly. However, staff perceived that
this was not 'normal' behaviour and, thus, it was deemed to be
'inappropriate':

They also knew that those people concerned enjoyed industrial work, and they could prove it.
(Carnie, 1990, p. 139)

The irony is that these adults, in rejecting the centre, made a
decision which led some of them into employment. Their actions
were not seen as indications of empowerment but as a basis for
offending the professionals involved. As Carnie recognised:

Professional people should try to avoid being defensive.
(Carnie, 1990, p. 139)

In a relationship of unequals, the task of translating rhetoric into
practice will always be contentious.

LIMITATIONS OF CHOICE

One of our concerns is to provide an antidote to those approaches which offer a non-problematic view of the world. This
must not be interpreted as an indifference to individual rights.
It is, rather, a recognition of the fundamental structural, ideological and economic factors which constitute formidable
barriers to change. This requires government support and investment, changes in legislation and the creation of a barrier-free
society, including addressing the conditions of the work place.
The economic and power relations supporting this structure
have to be challenged. This necessitates more than a programme

which depicts the tasks mainly in terms of individual attitudes and skills.

Facing such complex issues, we believe it to be politically naive to underestimate the profundity of the difficulties involved and the struggle required. We see it as morally unacceptable to simplify what is a complex and contentious process. Vulnerable groups must not be made more vulnerable by the imposition of idealised and romantic views of the world, no matter how worthy the intentions. Such simplified forms of discourse are essentially fraudulent and counter-productive to the cause of significant change.

Examples of the limitations of choice are important in setting the struggle for change within a material context. An initial barrier for students in wheelchairs is physical access. Many FE colleges will enrol only a restricted number of students in relation to their current resources (Barnard and Linehan, 1989). Issues like adequate toileting arrangements can take priority over academic choices. In a world in which the market is encouraging competition between institutions for student places, expensive structural alterations are unlikely to be made, particularly where the authorities believe there are few students involved. A dichotomy has arisen in that the establishment of certain FE colleges as offering exceptional access has allowed others to abdicate responsibility. This has inevitably restricted choice.

Special education has been recognised as containing a disproportionate number of working-class children and young people (Barton, 1986 and Tomlinson, 1982). The lives of young people defined as having moderate learning difficulties have often been complicated by poor housing and poverty (Hamilton, 1989). In her description of student progress in an inner-city area, Wilkinson (1990) emphasises their experience of domestic instability and living conditions in which 'they would always be either sharing a room or sleeping in the living room. The flats were cold and damp and the area boasted one of the highest rates of TB in the country' (p. 34). Such experiences cannot but influence the degree to which college can offer real choices. Even the decision to come to college in the first place was unlikely to have been theirs alone:

Referred to college by teachers, careers or social services

and encouraged by families who did not want them hanging around the house, it is not always the decision the young person might have made. However, their choice is limited and their chances of finding employment are low. Faced with this, college may well be seen as better than nothing, especially if they are eligible for any income, grant or trainee allowance.

(Wilkinson, 1990, p. 35)

Many of these young people are those with moderate learning difficulties who live in areas of high unemployment or underemployment. As a group, they reflect marked regional differences in opportunities and demonstrate the importance of socio-economic factors. Serious journalism is beginning to recognise the gravity of this situation, as can be seen in the following comments on the plight of such young people.

Education is the only way out of a vicious spiral in which a job is just a harder way of staying poor. But these communities have no tradition of further education. Over the last 10 years even the apprenticeships have disappeared, to be replaced by the universally loathed Training Schemes, which are widely dismissed – by parents and young people – as scab-labour jobs: depressing wage levels and distorting the supply of local labour. . . . On these estates truancy levels are high and academic achievement regarded as alien. As a free market develops in education, these youngsters are stuck in the bargain basement.

(Phillips, 1990, p. 4)

This reflection reiterates earlier contentions (e.g. Barton, 1986; Tomlinson, 1982) that the relationship between socio-economic factors and educational stigma is both endemic and progressive.

CONCLUSION

In offering these various examples of choices restricted by disability, class and cultural factors, we are seeking to emphasise the difficulties involved in any move for change. The lives of marginalised groups are inevitably influenced by the degree to which they are able to engage in any form of social, educational and economic participation. Factors such as the constraints of physical barriers, the impact of prejudice and the isolating effects of poverty will critically inhibit educational and employment opportunities. Challenging such inequities is a constituent of 'normalisation' for these are part of people's real experiences:

> Today, the idea of normalisation reaches to many of the public, social and education services for children, the elderly, persons with handicaps and others who require special assistance. The idea is similar to the basis of democracy, solidarity and egalitarianism. It should be promoted by economic and social security, equality of living conditions and active participation in community life.
>
> (Katoda and Miron, 1990, p. 134)

Creating such a basis for normalisation requires fundamental political changes beyond the scope of individuals. Yet, the curriculum for students with special needs in further education has traditionally presented an individualised model for transition to adult life. This description of one college's provision is typical:

> All courses are designed to enable students to make a successful transition to adult and working life. Independence and coping skills, self-advocacy, problem-solving and self-reliance, language development and communication skills are keys to this transition. Travel experience, work placements and residential visits help to foster the individual and social skills required for adult life.
>
> (College programme, 1989)

Such an emphasis sounds positive. The concept of 'self' is prominently figured, suggesting that successful transition is in the control of the individual. However, we would maintain that this is far from the case and that such an inference is oppressive in itself as it fails to acknowledge the impact of external forces.

In the next chapter, we will examine the development of the special curriculum in further education. We will look at those economic and social factors which have shaped this provision and at the skills-based model which was adopted. Neither the curriculum nor the teaching methods which were promoted are context-free. Both relate to the role and status of marginalised young people.

The curriculum for young people and adults with special educational needs is influenced by demographic shifts and the national changes imposed by innovations such as NVQs (Unwin, 1990). It is also related to LEA and college policy, as courses for special needs are rarely profit-making and 'it may be necessary for the College to invest heavily in making possible an efficient, profitable income-generating operation, so that such subsidising of the non-income bearing provision is made possible' (Bagley, 1988, p. 85). The vulnerability of special needs courses, as the 'poor relations' of FE provision, reveals the contradictions and tensions in the use of individualised models of empowerment and advocacy. Empowerment from a fragile power base can only foster frustration.

QUESTIONS FOR DISCUSSION

1 What presumptions about 'normality' are contained in the notion of adulthood?
2 Do you regard it as a professional duty or intrusion to conflate the public and private spheres of disabled people's lives?
3 In this chapter, can we be accused of deliberately complicating and politicising what should be an essentially practical issue?

3

CURRICULUM ISSUES

In this chapter we will focus upon recent curriculum frameworks designed for students with special educational needs in FE. These include a preparation for employment for students with moderate learning difficulties, a training in social skills for students with severe learning difficulties and a programme for community living which includes students with complex difficulties. As we stated in our introduction, our intention is not to elaborate upon details of curricular and teaching approaches, but to set curriculum issues into a broader context and, by so doing, challenge certain assumptions.

All educational institutions are involved in a social practice. The curriculum they offer is selected from a range of existing knowledge. It is organised in particular ways and employed for pre-defined purposes. As such, it is not divorced from the perceived needs of society. Curricular knowledge, therefore, involves values, priorities and moral commitments which Apple (1990) describes as 'oughtness and goodness'. This is reflected, for example, in the fostering of enterprise as a central curricular component. The National Curriculum Guidance on *Education for Citizenship* (1990) recommends that an area of study might include 'the importance to society and the individual of wealth creation, work and leisure' (p. 8). Thus the good citizen is the one who actively contributes to the economic well-being of society. Where does this leave those who, by no fault of their own, are unable to compete, participate in and enjoy the fruits of their labours? As disabled people recognise, their dependent social status as recipients of charity devalues them, existing in a citizenship on the margins (Lumb, 1990).

In the further education area, more than any other, the need to present a social, political and economic contextualising of educational issues is paramount. Three key aspects of curricular concern for young people with special educational needs can be identified as those we have selected to examine: a preparation for employment; a social skills training; a programme for living in the community. None of these aspects should be seen in a social vacuum. As we have emphasised, youth employment opportunities are influenced by marked geographical differences and national economic developments, social skills training is shaped by and relates to cultural norms and prevailing attitudes and community participation is reliant upon government priorities, available resources and levels of public awareness.

Whilst we remain convinced of the necessity of our approach, some of our readers may still feel that education and politics are separate issues and a political analysis, therefore, is inappropriate. We would contend that such a division is both untenable and unhelpful, particularly as explicit political interference is evident in the content and prioritising within the National Curriculum and other features of the Education Reform Act 1988 (Hargreaves, 1989; Flude and Hammer, 1990; Whitty, 1989). The contextualising of curricular issues prompts us to ask a number of questions.

- Whose perceptions of the needs of society are significant?
- Why is knowledge structured in a particular way?
- How is achievement measured and recognised and whose purpose does the curriculum serve?

In thinking about questions of this nature it is important to distinguish between curricular rhetoric and the realities of daily practice. Practitioners themselves need to step back and evaluate the role they play, the extent to which their decisions are controlled by external forces and the level of pragmatism which forces them into often uncomfortable choices. Their control over the curriculum they teach may be significantly limited. Both internal and external politics determine the nature of the curriculum. Practitioners may be constrained by factors beyond their control as well as influenced by their own preconceptions.

PREPARATION FOR EMPLOYMENT

Programmes in FE for students with moderate learning difficulties have had, as one of their basic aims, a preparation for employment (Bradley, 1985). The influence of economic factors on this type of curriculum is readily acknowledged:

> Because of the changing nature of the labour market and the introduction of new technologies individuals must be prepared to move into different kinds of work. . . . They must be adaptable, both when seeking their first employment and in meeting the changing demands that may characterise their future work.
>
> (Bradley, 1985, p. 16)

The emphasis here is on strengthening the possibilities for employment through responsible individual action in the form of continued adaptability. However, as Griffiths (1989) illustrates, the changing nature of the labour market places young people with learning difficulties at the periphery of employment opportunities. Thus, in addition to adaptability, these young people are expected to become more marketable through the demonstration of presentable behaviours. Work preparation courses are often presented as a series of behavioural objectives (Daniels, 1990). It is not skills but personal attributes which are assessed. In the highly influential *Skills for Living* (FEU, 1982), for example, a curricular aim is 'To present themselves well' which includes washing with soap, brushing teeth, selecting clothes and keeping them cleaned and ironed (p. 24). This intensive focus on presentation reflects the true nature of adaptability demanded in an increasingly competitive context. 'Skills' have little bearing on employability at this level. Where competition for unskilled work is fierce, a clean and tidy appearance becomes one favourable facet which might facilitate selection. No amount of good individual performance at a highly skilled level will ever compensate for necessary investment and economic development in a particular region.

The recognition of such external factors appears to become anaesthetised from the consciousness of the creators of curriculum programmes in their translation to objectives. This depoliticising and individualising of curriculum packages has to be understood in relation to changing demands in further education. In a climate where increasing numbers of mainstream lecturers are being asked to include students with learning difficulties in pre-vocational courses, accessible and simplified curriculum objectives are seen as pragmatically essential, of immediate value and fulfilling short-term goals. Managing the difficulties involved in teaching marginalised groups can often mean shelving wider and unavoidably complex issues. Although we understand the reasons why practitioners adopt this position, we feel that the struggle for social justice will be inhibited by a strict adherence to this narrow view of practical concerns. This type of focus lends itself more easily to a deficit view of these students. Practitioners need to resist any approach which reinforces feelings of inadequacy in students by placing the onus on *them* rather than *society* to change.

Much of the FEU literature on curriculum developments for students with learning difficulties has presented a skills-based model and, we would argue, an approach quite divorced from political conflicts and tensions within further education and beyond. However, more general FEU documents both recognise and evaluate the impact of external forces on curricular provision:

> What an LEA chooses to provide will be determined by its political character, by the strength of its industry, by its values as a provider of equal opportunities or its past record in education, by the amount of money it is prepared to put into its schools and colleges, and by its geographical character. Coming from the colleges will be plans based on many of the same determinants.
>
> (Kedney and Parkes, 1988, p. 62)

There is also an evident sensitivity to the social and economic context from which, for example, unemployed adult learners are drawn:

> It became impossible to separate the academic guidance and support from broader social and personal issues. Questions about state benefits, health matters, housing issues – in fact the whole range of issues which face the long-termed unemployed – were raised, and a policy decision regarding the role of college staff had to be taken.
>
> (Wallace, 1990, p. 7)

The marked contrast between the sophisticated level of debate engaged in within a broad further education context and the severely restricted parameters of discussion related to the special needs area is indicative of the way in which this aspect has been depoliticised and undertheorised.

TRAINING IN SOCIAL SKILLS

A social skills training for students with learning difficulties or disabilities is seen as an essential component of their preparation for adulthood. The fundamental purpose of this training is to groom these young people for assimilation into society. Underpinning such programmes is a tacit understanding of what constitutes 'normal' adulthood. The social skills identified as significant in training packages have usually been decontextualised with little regard for cultural diversity. In addition, the selection of specific tasks can encourage the adoption of outmoded and stereotypical behaviours and habits, rather than allow for spontaneity and individuality.

Tasks have tended to be presented in an artificially complicated format in order both to break them down into simplified steps and to present a challenging programme. For example, Whelan and Speake (1979) 'list the basic steps involved in tying a simple knot in a neck-tie' (p. 97) in thirty-one separate stages. Whilst we recognise that such a programme reflects now outdated concepts of 'normality', it is important to ask how objectives are established, on what basis, and whose priorities take precedence? The social skills programme has moved from schools into FE. There has been an inevitable time-lag in which aspects of the college curriculum now need a radical reappraisal. Ainscow (Ainscow and Tweddle, 1979, 1984, 1988) has made a significant contribution to this area of curriculum development. His redefinition of priorities, in reflecting on his own changing objectives, has led him to challenge former strategies of task analysis (Ainscow, 1991). This challenge needs to be addressed in the FE special curriculum, if it is to offer objectives which promote empowerment and recognise differences.

Generally, the essential components of a social skills programme are daily living tasks such as cleaning, shopping, cooking, washing and ironing clothes. Whilst we acknowledge that most adults engage in such activities to a greater or lesser degree, the extent to which they become a major priority is affected by a wide range of social factors. For those who can afford to pay others to do these chores, other skills will take priority. Therefore, social and economic circumstances shape the degree to which certain tasks will be viewed as necessary. Not having to undertake such chores, far from diminishing adult status, can be seen as a symbol of high social standing. One of the dangers of such programmes is that they encourage a social rigidity in the lives of vulnerable groups. Part of this rigidity is the curbing of spontaneity and choice.

A mother of a young woman with Down's Syndrome, for example, recognises the tensions inherent in her daughter's natural spontaneity. When she dances in a shopping precinct, to the delight of other shoppers, her mother realises that this would not meet with the approval of her college tutors, who would regard this behaviour as inappropriate. She contends that

> Intensive training programmes to teach socially acceptable behaviour can, if pushed too far, result in the suppression of spontaneous expression, the negation of personality.
>
> (West, 1986, p. 12)

Support, in the social training of vulnerable young people, treads a delicate line between controlling and empowering. Too often, the rhetoric may be empowerment but the results are control. In order to foster the empowerment, staff must contend with inevitable difficulties, conflicts and confusions as they guide learners, unfamiliar with decision-making, through the process of change. Sutcliffe (1990) recognises the dilemma for staff and the natural temptation to retain the familiar patterns of control and management. True empowerment involves the redefining of social values, extending the boundaries of what constitutes 'appropriate' behaviour and accepting a wider range of cultural differences.

COMMUNITY LIVING

For those of us who take living in the community for granted, a training for community living seems superfluous. Preparation for community living can involve young people moving from special schools into FE colleges and beyond or older people moving out of long-stay hospitals. For both groups, essential needs are seen as highly complex:

> What are the learning needs of people who are embarking on the first steps to an ordinary life? We see them as making choices, making decisions, personal care, domestic skills, leisure and recreational skills, human relationships, an understanding of the locality, appropriate basic skills, including literacy, numeracy, budgeting and oracy, personal creativity, health and nutrition.
>
> (Crook, 1988, p. 7)

This focus upon choice and skills implies that, with an acquisition of appropriate tools, community living will be accessible. We would challenge this assumption and contend that societal attitudes and public services can mitigate against fulfilling community involvement. What constitutes an 'ordinary life' is contentious. It is not merely a matter of displaying skills but rather of owning a social role. The form and degree of ownership will be sharply defined by individual experiences of social conditions and relationships. Economic status, to a considerable extent, will determine the level of community involvement which is within the control of an individual.

At the most basic level, community living has to offer housing of some kind. The 'care in the community' initiative has not enjoyed a smooth passage. Recent newspaper coverage indicates that only 22 per cent of the general public wholeheartedly welcome this move with over half the stories dwelling on the failures (Wertheimer, 1988). An example, in *The Independent* of 22 November 1990, shows citizens in expensive suburban areas resisting the inclusion of former residents of long-stay hospitals, suggesting 'that placements should be made only on council estates' (Roe, 1990, p. 20). Such responses reflect attitudes towards social status. Ownership of a social role involves specific economic symbols relating to property rights. Where success is measured by the quality of housing, the inclusion of vulnerable, and (some might add) undeserving, groups is difficult. For young people whose complex physical disabilities require a high level of care, the key aim of their college training is that of finding an appropriate, or at least an adequate, placement (Corbett, 1991). In both instances, the issue of placement becomes a goal in itself. Yet, placement in the community does not constitute participation.

If the community is to include even very difficult and potentially disruptive members, it has to be able to offer extremely flexible and imaginative service support (Blunden and Allen, 1987). However, provision like that offered by national voluntary organisations can be resistant to change and ill-equipped to respond flexibly for

> Even relatively straightforward changes can founder because of a lack of infrastructure for introducing change of any kind in a systematic manner.
>
> (Connelly, 1990, p. 37)

Parents of young people with disabilities can also be resistant to change, cautious of exposing their children to risks (Dee, 1988). Thus choice, within the context of limited services and parental pressures, should not focus upon skills alone. It has to involve more imaginative opportunities, as Atkinson and Brechin (1989) recognise when they ask students in their *Patterns for Living* course to reflect upon things they have never tried before and to 'start exploring possibilities and sharing ideas' (p. 57). This shared involvement relates to the advocacy movement and the mutual support it offers (Richardson and Ritchie, 1989). Yet, Dowson (1990) suggests that it must develop further to 'become an ordinary, everyday activity – so ordinary that it ceases to need a special label' (p. 10). Until it reaches that stage, self-advocacy remains a veneer of empowerment with professionals still stage-managing the action, in which self-advocates are compelled to perform to their maximum level under a public spotlight and critical scrutiny.

Service providers are becoming increasingly sensitive to client needs and seek to encourage flexible provision (Seed and Montgomery, 1989). This includes enabling people to use a range of services, like day centres, as and when they want them and to get support to build their own domestic lives as they wish. Such an emphasis is surely preferable to the prevalent focus on training programmes, for

> People with learning difficulties are very often forced to engage in endless training. They can spend an entire

'working' life being 'educated and trained' at a day centre. Even at home they may be expected to do training in order to move towards independence.

(Dowson, 1990, p. 16)

Dowson's comments reiterate our earlier criticisms of a distinctive pathway to adulthood for marginalised groups. Training, in the abstract, is no substitute for living.

CONCLUSION

The curriculum provided for young people with disabilities and learning difficulties is centred around the promotion of those skills deemed necessary in their future adult lives. These basic needs relate to the nature of their prospective employment or occupational activities, their role in society and the contribution they are expected to make as citizens.

In this chapter, we asked how achievement was measured and recognised and whose purpose was served by the curriculum. To a considerable extent, achievement is measured through competitive assessment which is further fostered in the National Curriculum. This places the most vulnerable young people at the lowest level when they leave school to seek potential employment, training or further education. Learning to be flexible and compliant as employees are their most marketable assets within this context.

In the following chapter we will examine the experiences and opportunities which some young people find in their quest for training in vocational skills. For some of them, the Youth Training (YT) programme is a welcome contrast with their experience of failure at school and an environment which promotes their self-esteem. Yet, even those same young people who find some value in their YT experience will often acknowledge that it is exploitative and is only an acceptable alternative to the dole. In exploring the training procedures for this most vulnerable group, we intend to reflect the ambivalence they often feel, the difficulties both they and their instructors can experience and the painful gap which exists between their aspirations and the actual choices available to them.

QUESTIONS FOR DISCUSSION

1 In what ways can social skills programmes encourage diversity and choice?
2 Should programmes be concerned with raising issues of conflict and prejudice?
3 How valid is the authors' contention that social justice is a fundamental issue in relation to this topic?

4

VOCATIONALISM
Experiences and opportunities

A central component in the further education curriculum for
students with learning difficulties or disabilities is 'a preparation
for employment'. This period of preparation has changed during the 1980s. Where many low-achievers from secondary
schools, and even school leavers from special schools for pupils
with moderate learning difficulties, had formerly gone from
school into work at 16, large-scale youth unemployment halted
this progression. As a direct consequence, many young people
retained their 'special need' label into further education and
training programmes. There was no unskilled work for them.
Therefore, they had to learn those skills they needed. For many
FE lecturers and YT trainers, this meant trying to cope with
uncomfortable and often resentful students who had failed at
school and sought jobs, not training.

The relationship between schooling and work has been a
perennial cause for concern throughout the history of state
provision of schools. Its meaning and significance has taken
different forms during particular historical moments, such as
growing youth unemployment or recession. The impact of this
concern has been differentially experienced, with pupils being
separated into vocational or academic courses. The discourse
legitimising such practices has, as Holt maintains:

a simple, cracker-barrel appeal; make schools more vocational so that their products may be more employable and
our economy more competitive.

(Holt, 1990, Introduction)

This perspective has a specific interpretation of work in occupational terms.

Within our society work is not only the central means by which people earn a living, but also an identity-shaping process. To be 'normal' is to work and young people not involved in full-time employment are seen as a problem and/or a potential menace to political stability (Borsay, 1986).

Pay is a status symbol and a means of existence. Its importance is enhanced when one recognises that workers are also consumers. Thus, Fraser maintains:

> Lack of money, where money is the socially validated measure of all human activity and worth, is a derogative of a person's possibilities, a human lack.
>
> (Fraser, 1969, p. 9)

Inequalities of access into the labour market and the differential pay rewards involved are significant legitimations of the social power of the wage. Thus, to be out of work involves social exclusion from one of the dominant forms of identity creation.

However, to suggest that work in any form is intrinsically beneficial, would be misleading. Some work contexts are alienating and de-humanising. The nature of the work itself effectively serves as an oppression and inhibitor to personal growth. Spours and Young (1988) suggest that we need to move towards a broader understanding and definition of work which includes the domestic sphere and leisure activities. This broad perspective would entail the right to choose not to engage in paid employment if it was considered inappropriate and unpalatable. However, most young people are not in a position to choose but to accept compromise. They have to enter Youth Training programmes if they leave school at 16 or they get no dole money. Other young people choose employment but have to settle for day centre provision as they are considered unemployable.

In this chapter, we will explore the struggle for choice in three main areas. Firstly, we examine the training for employment offered to young people with learning difficulties and disabilities and the extent to which it is an empowering process. Secondly, we look at ways in which young people are supported and sustained in finding and keeping employment. Thirdly, we examine alternatives to employment and the degree to which they offer choices.

TRAINING FOR EMPLOYMENT

Young people with learning difficulties and disabilities are included in the Youth Training programme, both in discrete provision and in integrated schemes. Cooper (1988) has provided guidance to employers and instructors in training programmes which emphasise the individual requirements of specific trainees and the way in which programmes can accommodate them. Her focus on meeting individual needs, however, fails to address the broader issues of discrimination on the grounds of race, gender and disability. Training for employment is not about recognising individual need but about responding to economic and political change. This is illustrated in the current insecurity within such programmes. While YTS was launched as an essential process of skills training, it is now being dissolved in certain areas which find it no longer useful:

> Uptake of YT reflects local labour market conditions: where the economy is buoyant YT has become an irrelevance. In London and the South East many employers, especially small firms, have gone back to their traditional methods of recruitment by word of mouth and informal training on the job, even if they are still subsidised by YT, while many large employers have formally opted-out of the scheme. Even in Sheffield the large council-run and subsidised scheme has now more or less collapsed.
>
> (Ainley, 1990, p. 40)

In many prosperous areas, Youth Training (YT) has remained as a provision largely serving the most disadvantaged and those with special training needs. Yet, this cannot be seen as an ideological development for it is subject to sudden changes in relation to altered economic circumstances. Thus, whilst in 1989 Cambridgeshire offered Employment Training (ET) for trainees with special needs as its employment rate was high generally, when, in 1990, there were many redundancies in local industries the ET provision was immediately changed to cater exclusively for the more employable casualties of this new economic change.

Since its inception, the ET programme has included those people who for various reasons were unlikely to gain open employment yet, if the Training and Enterprise Councils (TECs) are to perform as selectors of viable initiatives, this development will be threatened by 'creaming off higher quality training for the employed, abandoning lower levels and the unemployed at whom TA/MSC programmes were previously aimed' (Ainley, 1990, p. 12). Young people with special educational needs were the last to be included in training programmes but appear to be the first group to be seen as expendable.

EMPOWERING FOR EMPLOYMENT

For young people from special schools, the training for employment has to include an element of compensatory education which Griffiths (1989) refers to as 'The empowering curriculum'. He suggests that young people with disabilities need to have an opportunity for decision-making, risk-taking, self-advocacy and 'freedom for adolescent behaviour' (p. 19). The latter element is particularly relevant in relation to equal opportunities in that expectations made of students with disabilities and learning difficulties often force unreasonable responsibilities upon them:

> People with learning difficulties are often expected to 'jump through hoops' and to be ultra-perfect at everyday chores before being given the chance to be more independent.
>
> (Sutcliffe, 1990, p. 79)

Yet, as Griffiths stresses, a specially designed curriculum for employment must not become divorced from the realities of the outside world. In a Youth Training Workshop which promoted an equal opportunities policy, for example, a young woman trainee in a wheelchair was encouraged to complete a carpentry training option, despite the fact that the instructor had to do all the physical tasks for her (Corbett, 1990). Whilst she was not being prevented from choosing what she wanted, she was not being confronted with the external pressures which would really determine employment choices.

The actual requirements of employers, when interviewed about their experience of employing people with a disability, appear to be quite specific. They constitute an 'Employability Package', which includes reliability, conscientiousness and commitment as key factors (Griffiths, 1989). Such an emphasis indicates that attitudes rather than skills are seen as central factors. If this is the case, then learning difficulties should prove no barrier to employment. However, some young people with learning difficulties find that sustaining regular work patterns is extremely difficult and they fail to keep jobs which have been found for them. It might be suggested that they had been given the choice but had simply not coped. Once again, their individual deficiencies could be blamed for their apparent unemployability. Where sustained support is provided until the individual is settled into a work pattern, this can have excellent results (Williams, 1991). For the young man offered in this example, supporting him into employment meant that he felt

A lot happier and contented, generally wanted. I was told at the rehabilitation centre that I was unemployable. I have proved to myself and others that I am employable.
(quoted in Williams, 1991, p. 4)

Some recent schemes have illustrated that even those young people 'excluded on the grounds of "challenging behaviour" from special schools and day centres' (Sutcliffe, 1990, p. 73) have the capacity to sustain jobs if they are given adequate support.

Sutcliffe (1990) describes how, in a Social Services Scheme at Blakes Wharf run by Hammersmith and Fulham, a team of six employment advisers support people with learning difficulties in not only finding but, more critically, keeping the right job. They have met with notable success but Sutcliffe recognises the highly intensive staff input which is required in order to provide systematic instruction. Perhaps this example typifies the dilemma of creating choice for a marginalised group. Whilst intensive teaching of new job skills in work settings has to be given and only gradually faded out if people are to gain the confidence to sustain real jobs, this labour intensive process is surely vulnerable in an enterprise culture. The extent to which Employment Training (ET) can support people into real job opportunities may depend on the degree to which such provision is seen as a viable enterprise by the TECs.

THE ILLUSION OF SUPPORT

For young people with physical and sensory disabilities, the development of increasingly sophisticated technology might appear to offer access to training and employment. Yet, recent research indicates that whilst those with access to IT could compete in open employment just like anyone else, there is actually hardly any provision for employment-related aids between school and work (Vincent, 1989). The benefits of advanced technology to disabled people have been largely illusory:

> Despite the IT revolution and the findings of the Coopers and Lybrand report 'Information Needs of Disabled People, Their Carers and Service Providers' (DHSS, 1988) computerized databases are still a distant goal for most service providers. Lack of finance is a constant refrain although available evidence points to lack of co-ordination between departments and the need for clear goals. Consider the fact that last year disabled youngsters leaving school did not benefit from £50 million extra government funding earmarked for them. The main reason was that local and central government had not agreed on how to use the funds.
>
> (Vincent, 1989, p. 281)

The notion of a struggle for choice seems apposite in this context. Contradictions abound. The above funds were not received by those who needed them although they were quite specifically made available in order to comply with clauses in the Disabled Persons Act 1986. These funds were seen as crucial in supporting disabled young people in their transition to further education, training, employment and independent living. Financial resources at this critical stage would make all the difference between autonomy and dependency. Coupled with this dichotomy between apparent legislation and what Vincent (1989) terms an 'almost catatonic inability by officials to translate policy into action' (p. 281) is the ineffectiveness of the employment Quota Scheme. An indication of the ludicrous nature of this system, designed to ensure some element of positive discrimination for disabled employees, is that the number of employers complying with it has dropped from 53 per cent in 1965 to 27 per cent in

1986, while 56 per cent of employers have special permits relieving them of any commitment to meet the quota. As Vincent suggests:

> No problem here of matching the disabled person's aspirations to what is available.
>
> (Vincent, 1989, p. 281)

The element of choice in such a discriminatory context is clearly significantly restricted. Thus, disabled young people have to be either super-heroes to conquer these obstacles and achieve a degree of status and independence or else they are positively encouraged into a resigned passivity.

CUSHIONED FROM REALITY

A reflection of the marginalised identity of young people with disabilities and learning difficulties is that they are often perceived as virtually invisible such that professionals are expected to speak on their behalf. For example, within one training programme for vulnerable young people, staff defined their role as acting 'as an impartial advocate to look after their interests' which included intervening in bias and harassment (Corbett, 1990, p. 90). Whilst undoubtedly well-motivated, such paternalism serves to shape what are perceived as unacceptable behaviours rather than challenge the status quo. Vulnerable and uncomfortable trainees have to be packaged and sold to employers. This attitude is rejected by an employment service called **WORKLINK** which supports its disabled clients in becoming active participants in their assessment:

> **WORKLINK** is not in the business of 'selling disabled people to employers'. They seek to avoid the traditional approach whereby a professional promotes employment on behalf of a disabled person, acting as the contact with the employer; they see this as creating a sense of dependency. Instead, clients are encouraged to gain a realistic knowledge of their abilities in relation to real jobs.
>
> (Newman, 1990, p. 51)

This emphasis on *realistic* knowledge and *real* jobs is critical if paternalism is to be avoided. In this context, the young woman in a wheelchair doing carpentry which is done for her by an instructor can be seen only as a token. She is not being offered realistic experience for real choice. Protection from reality cannot be supported under a truly empowering curriculum for employment. Removal of the cushioned buffer can be seen as harsh. Integration is challenging and difficult. It exposes vulnerable groups to the competitive market, where the failure of a certain proportion is inevitable.

ALTERNATIVES – A VIABLE OPTION?

Disabled people are not a homogeneous group. Some of them have complex and multiple disabilities. The parameters of their choices will be mediated through these personal factors. For some, employment may not appear a viable option. Training for them involves a preparation for living without paid work. This does not preclude them, however, from a struggle for choice. In this instance it is a choice of community living. Whereas, in the past, young people with severe and complex disabilities would have automatically proceeded into life-long residential care, they are now encouraged to select from various options. This could include sheltered housing with whatever support they require, hostel living and a range of independent living projects in which they are offered opportunities for choice in daily living.

This move to extend choice can be seen as empowering for young people whose lives are severely restricted by extreme dependency. However, empowerment carries responsibilities with it which can sometimes seem onerous. It is stressful for all adolescents to learn to cope with taking risks, making decisions and accepting the consequences. They usually have a gradual progression into this process through an intermittent sequence of increasingly more difficult choices over a number of years. For young people with severe disabilities, opportunities to express choice and to experience adventure are influenced by the initiative and priorities of their carers. This means that their skills at decision-making may have remained under-developed.

The ability to make choices involves a learning process. There is no such thing as absolute independence. There are choices for degrees of dependency. These young people have every right to decide that they would prefer a high level of care in order to pursue alternatives to daily living skills. However, if they wish to define how that care should be delivered to meet their specific requirements, they are unlikely to have control over service provision as

> disabled people are offered little choice about aids and equipment, times at which professionals can attend to help with matters like toileting, dressing or preparing a meal are restricted, and the limited range of tasks that professionals can perform are further limited because of professional boundaries, employer requirements or trade union practices.
>
> (Oliver, 1989, p. 13)

Choice, therefore, is set within a constricted service in which clients have to conform to what professionals can offer. The dominance of certain professional bodies, particularly those in the medical and related professions, has led to a focus on individual need and to the legitimation of a model of care which allows minimal control by the recipients (Barton, 1989).

Where empowerment has been exercised to the extent of enabling residents in homes for disabled people to select and dismiss carers on their own criteria for the quality of service they require, this can create considerable stress and hostility, testing the strength of residents to the utmost. As always, real empowerment is extremely exacting, challenging and demands cool nerve. The very professionals who ostensibly foster empowerment may be the first to be rejected when it really emerges. They need to be prepared for this. If disabled people are to take control of their own lives, this will inevitably involve an uncomfortable renegotiation of terms with their carers. As Barnes (1990) noted, some disabled people will retreat into apathy rather than risk this whilst others complain but are cautious of changing relationships with those who, despite a rhetoric of empowerment, have control over their lives. It takes confidence to assume an autonomous status and few disabled people have been provided with opportunities to develop self-esteem and feelings of genuine power to manage their personal agenda.

QUALITY OF LIVING

For people with learning difficulties, moving into the community, their network of relationships may be fragile and based largely on former acquaintanceships from school or hospital. Building and sustaining relationships is a complex and intricate process, yet one which is fundamental to a genuine participation within a community (Richardson and Ritchie, 1989; Firth and Rapley, 1990). Despite living in homes within the community, some people with learning difficulties make few new friends in the residential provision with even fewer beyond it:

> The relative paucity of friendships and close if not intimate relationship among those with learning difficulties is neither coincidental nor accidental. So frequently repeated a phenomenon of apparent social exclusion has to be seen as the result of social processes. It is such processes, we argue, that the call to 'make community living real' has overlooked.
>
> (Evans and Murcott, 1990, p. 129)

The social stigma of disability, whilst possibly masked in superficial contacts, is revealed when the issue of sustained friendship is addressed. The elaborate guidelines offered by Firth and Rapley (1990) to promote skills for developing friendship are addressed to people with learning difficulties and their carers. It is for them to work at relationships: they, not other people, need to make the effort. Invariably, if people with disabilities and learning difficulties are to enjoy active participation in their communities where they do not already have status and identity through playing a specific role in that arena, the ability to adapt and comply has to come from them.

Finding suitable living accommodation, if you are in a wheelchair, can be fraught with frustration. Choice usually ends in compromise. Unless we listen to the experiences of disabled people, we will not understand the reality of what community living can entail. Prolonged and repeated disappointments and humiliations not only can influence the way people behave but also can affect their whole attitude to life, souring their expectations:

Unsuitable living accommodation can turn a disabled person into a prisoner in their own home, denied access to the outside world and forced to depend on others. It is literally a living nightmare for a person to be unable to get out of the house without help or, especially for those who are incontinent, to have difficulty getting to a bathroom. I know from bitter experience the feelings of helplessness and shame such frustrations can generate. The whole life of a disabled person can revolve around getting to the toilet in time, and the psychological pressure can be intense. It turns a disability into an unbearable handicap, and can totally distort the personality.

(Davis, 1989, pp. 27–8)

For many young people with disabilities or learning difficulties, their only realistic choice is to remain living with their parents in an environment in which they have learnt to cope. In the 'Care in the Community' initiative it is again the family, and specifically the mother, who is expected to take on the caring. Feminist critics have alerted us to the unfair demands this places upon women, within

the pervasive ideology of possessive individualism which increasingly dominates contemporary political thinking – at the expense of collectivist values which might offer a greater source of support and concern both for women and for those who are dependent on structured forms of care.

(Dalley, 1989, p. 205)

However, Keith (1992), herself a disabled woman, rejects the notion that caring for disabled people is an unreasonable burden but suggests that it can be viewed as part of a reciprocal relationship. Another disabled woman (Begum, 1990) supports this perspective in emphasising the complexity of a caring partnership, both carer and cared-for benefiting from a valued reciprocity which enhances quality of life. If the only choice available is to live without paid employment, then the quality of that 'living' becomes of critical importance.

We would not wish to deny the considerable improvements now provided for people with disabilities and learning difficulties and the impact for good which the self-advocacy movement has achieved. However, social and economic inequalities miti-gate against this group – poor, dependent and sometimes regarded as a burden – becoming empowered at anything other than a superficial level.

CONCLUSION

The young people whose experiences have been discussed in this chapter form a marginalised but highly diverse group. They range from those students leaving comprehensive schools at 16 with no formal qualifications to young people who are progress-ing from special schooling into residential special college provision. Some may simply be seen as low-achievers. Others are totally physically dependent or have difficulties in learning which have confined them within a restricted curriculum. Their experience of vocational training and the opportunities this offers will be correspondingly varied, influenced by a wide range of factors.

Within the discourse on vocationalism a number of tensions are apparent. These include a belief that current training policy is a further means of government intentions to control a poten-tial labour force set against the argument that such vocational reforms are long overdue in providing a more relevant curricu-lum (Ainley, 1988; Gleeson, 1989). The experiences of the young people concerned reflect both aspects of this discourse. The compulsory nature of Youth Training (YT) provision has forced 16-year-old school leavers into schemes where their real choice of options are extremely limited and may be seen to have lo-wered rather than broadened their horizons (Shilling, 1989; Hollands, 1990). Yet, where their experiences of schooling have been negative and damaging to self-esteem, the inclusion of 'personal effectiveness' support in YT programmes can serve to counteract past failures (Parsons, 1990).

One of the critical factors to recognise, in relation to these tensions, is the wide disparity in the quality and status of differ-ent schemes and the implications this has for employment prospects:

If the main avenue to employment offered by YTS is through being retained by a YTS employer, then selection at 16, to the 'right' scheme, remains critical. Selection on to the most sought-after YTS schemes, and the well-documented relation of ethnic, gender and social divisions to differentiation within YTS, will be lasting in their effects.

(Raffe, 1990, p. 54)

This issue achieves particular significance in relation to young people with disabilities and learning difficulties whose inclusion is ignored in this analysis. They are rarely placed on the most sought-after schemes with employers but are rather found in isolated workshop-based provision. Whilst agreeing with the levels of differentiation which the quotation highlights, we contend that trainees with learning difficulties and disabilities experience double discrimination.

If only the right schemes are likely to lead to employment, what is the purpose of training without jobs? Some trainees acknowledge the minimal skills input of schemes and have few expectations of them (Hollands, 1990). However, others are seduced by the language surrounding the notion of 'occupational competence' into anticipating unrealistic employment opportunities. The examples we have offered in this chapter have highlighted what we see as two fundamental issues. The first is that young people need real training for real jobs and this might mean confronting them with the extent of their limitations. The second is the need to determine and provide the level of sustained support necessary to help those who find a job to keep it.

We would not assume to underestimate the complexity of such an approach. It raises serious ethical dilemmas. If young people with disabilities and learning difficulties are to be supported in their struggle for choice, they are also to be allowed to experience risk, possible failure, stress and disappointment. It would be all too easy to retreat into cushioned passivity. For those young people who face multiple forms of discrimination, choice is vapid without a support structure. Where intentions have been expressed, a support system will provide a stronger possibility that they will be realised.

However, there are evident constraining factors inhibiting this development. It is extremely expensive and labour-intensive to provide this degree of support for what is a marginalised group. Within the terms of the enterprise culture, their contribution is superfluous. Questions of equity and social justice become insignificant. Many training programmes which were specifically designed to include trainees with disabilities and learning difficulties are now vulnerable to closure. The question of choice has to be set within real material conditions. Where those conditions are based on a premise of 'the survival of the fittest', this will inevitably restrict choice for the least vociferous. Choice depends upon power. Thus, for a relatively powerless group, choices are set within limited parameters.

Perhaps nowhere is this more evident than in planning for living in the community. In the next chapter, we will examine how a struggle for choice permeates all aspects of independent living.

QUESTIONS FOR DISCUSSION

1 If we recognise that employers discriminate on the grounds of race, gender and disability, to what extent can an empowering curriculum counteract this?
2 The issue of 'choice' is relative. Simple choices can be quantified. It is the more complex choices which are difficult. What would you suggest are the most important choices to address and why?
3 What disadvantages are there to the broad perspective the authors have adopted in this chapter? Can you argue for the merits of an alternative approach?

5

DIFFERENCES IN THE COMMUNITY

Colleges of Further Education are increasingly expected to be responsive to local community needs. They are also involved in the enterprise culture in which course provision and college organisation must be seen to be cost-effective. Achieving a satisfactory balance between these two often competing objectives can create tensions. Publicity about course provision may reach only certain segments within a community. For example, failure to attract black people on to courses can reflect an inadequate recruitment strategy. Recent research (FEU, 1987) suggested that

> There was little evidence of direct efforts to attract more black students to courses where they are currently under-represented. In general, it was implied that equality of opportunity meant offering the same opportunities and facilities to those who presented themselves, rather than considering structural inequities which might result in black students failing to meet the entry criteria. It was also not recognised in some cases that mainstream publicity might fail to reach the black community.
>
> (FEU, 1987, p. 5)

College responses to community needs, therefore, have to recognise differences within a community and to respond with flexibility.

Each local community has its distinctive character and particular history. Participation involves the interaction of people with different biographies, values and interests. In any attempt to gain an adequate understanding of the notion of 'community', issues of choice, power and status need to be addressed. The extent to which any community is enabling will be contingent upon established priorities, adequate resources, expectations and opportunities. The cruel realities of subordination and prejudice must not be glossed over in romantic concepts of 'community'.

In this chapter our discussion concerns those most marginalised and vulnerable members of the community, specifically young people with disabilities and learning difficulties. Such young people are generally placed on special courses in further education which, as we discussed earlier, tend to focus on providing functional skills for living successfully in the community. This practical element in now increasingly combined with an emphasis on empowerment. However, concepts of 'empowerment' and 'choice', whilst appealing to basic sentiments of equality, are difficult to translate into the context of a competitive and discrimatory society. This raises important questions, including:

- What does 'empowerment' mean in a community characterised by gross economic inequalities and prejudice?
- By what criteria do we define 'successful' living?

Addressing the issues of 'empowerment' and 'choice' is fundamental to the promotion of equality. By raising the above questions, we could be accused of replacing a positive rhetoric with a negative one. Our intention is not to denigrate the progress achieved in this area but to suggest that the complex issues involved cannot be fudged. Our respect for these young people as individuals compels us to confront the difficulties they are likely to face.

EMPOWERMENT AND INEQUALITY

Individual empowerment for disabled people is seen as a crucial vehicle for self-improvement. It is also presented as a means of developing relationships leading to wider social participation. This perspective is vividly illustrated by Fenton and Hughes (1989) when they maintain that 'the more self-empowered a person becomes, the more able s/he will be to enable others to be the same' (p. 19). The implications are that an internalised empowerment can alter external conditions. Individualised empowerment can promote group solidarity. However, its significance must be assessed in relation to the relative powerlessness of the group concerned.

What may be possible in one context may not be in another. Nor is it possible, through the development of the 'right attitudes', to merely think away powerful determinants such as economic inequalities. The hierarchical structures of organisations like colleges, with their different levels of power relations, should be a reminder of the limited scope of individual empowerment. Being able to be assertive with the lecturers for the special needs course, who may themselves command lowly status in the hierarchy, is one level of realisable empowerment. Even gaining access to the college principal, however, may be something else.

This focus on the need for individualised empowerment among disabled students illustrates the level of inequality they have to face. It is because they are a marginalised group that they have to struggle for control over basic features of their lives. This includes justifying their responses relating to personal issues generally kept within the private domain. As we examined in our discussion of 'Adulthood' (Chapter 2), Fenton and Hughes (1989) record a case conference in which a disabled student evaluates her inadequacies in social interaction. This aspect of personal development has become a core element of the curriculum for individualised empowerment. Yet, it would be peripheral to the curriculum of mainstream students. Similarly, in the example of social skills training offered in *From Coping to Confidence* (Bradley, 1985) students with learning difficulties are encouraged to critically examine their spontaneous behaviour. Such an approach fosters extreme self-consciousness and it can inhibit risk-permitted learning.

Brown (1988) calls for a more developed philosophy of transition and education. He suggests that these young people know their limitations all too well and that

Their inability to fulfil these needs probably has considerable relevance to the lack of development of positive self-image and probably has major implications for motivation and assertiveness. If one talks about transition

65

programs, one must also look to individual's concerns, worries and choices.

(Brown, 1988, p. 228)

An individualised model of empowerment, therefore, can be a reflection of devalued status and the stigma of difference within a community, rather than a recognition of limitations alone.

The effectiveness of promoting empowerment within special needs courses is muted by the low-status of this area of work in Further Education. A recent survey (FEU, 1990) found that

Time and again there was reference to the tenuous foot-hold which special needs work had within further education. As one co-ordinator observed: 'Usually, special needs is hanging by a thread within F. E.'

(FEU, 1990, p. 2)

This is an apt analogy in that the peripheral status of special needs in FE has historically annexed it from the mainstream. Special needs co-ordinators have largely been drawn from the special school sector. This has disadvantaged them in relation to becoming active participators in a complex political institution. As the FEU (1990) survey noted:

The most common remark made by managers about special needs staff was that they tended to be almost exclusively concerned with their specialism and did not fully understand 'how the F. E. system actually works'. As one head of department commented: 'They don't know their way around this institution . . . who to ask or the way to do it'.

(FEU, 1990, p. 2)

Empowerment is about participation in the establishing of priorities within an institution. Therefore, the extent to which the community of an FE college is enabling is contingent upon established priorities which will determine resourcing and expectations. Special needs co-ordinators have to learn their way around the FE system if they are to effect empowerment for themselves and, in turn, for their students.

A powerful illustration of the tensions between meeting community needs and cost-effectiveness is that of balancing improved access for disabled students and staff in FE against other competing priorities. As Turnham (1992), a special needs college co-ordinator, says:

> At the time of writing, recent plans to join two buildings with a walkway to improve access to the second building, which has no lift, have been scrapped. In the current financial climate, which sees us both wrestling with colleges managing their own budgets and, in our own authority, reeling from the outcome of 'poll capping', the expenses involved in improving physical access are likely to be vying alongside numerous other worthy but costly causes.
>
> (Turnham, 1992)

The unequal status of competing groups within this institutional community accentuates the vulnerability of individualised models of empowerment. Only when special needs is seen as part of an overall equal opportunity issue and where group solidarity is fostered can a marginalised status be challenged.

Students with special educational needs enter colleges from a range of different communities. These include social education centres, day centres, hospitals, special schools, mainstream schools, youth training and employment training programmes, hostels and domestic settings. That which constitutes a community within a single institution will, therefore, be complex and student experiences of social interaction similarly varied. Sometimes, the specific communities from which they come into college bear little relation to the general experience. As Taylor (1990) says:

> Think of a Day Centre you know. Think of the things which happen there. Are there things which happen which you could not quite *swear* are part of the weft and woof of everyday community life? Sometimes it is difficult to pin down what is odd. Perhaps it's the remarkable *powerlessness* which people have over their own lives. Or the confusion, the lack of purpose, the lack of *coherency*.
>
> (Taylor, 1990, p. 34)

Thus, the extent to which college courses can influence the development of empowerment for these individuals depends upon their previous experience and perceptions as well as the degree of institutional flexibility which they encounter. Their experiences of 'difference' in the wider community have resulted in isolation within that community. This isolation is often reinforced in the community of the FE college.

Often, college special needs courses, like Youth Training programmes, entail the combination of students from contrasting communities. Young people who have experienced difficulties in learning in comprehensive schools are placed in YT programmes alongside other young people from special schools. This challenge to staff can lead them to rely upon individualised learning models as the mixture of diverse needs mitigates against a corporate perspective on empowerment.

Geographical inequalities in relation to socio-economic factors are reflected in the working conditions and priorities within different institutions. The human and material resources are also affected. Different contexts offer contributing opportunities relating to both education and employment. In an exploration of how FE colleges meet the needs of the Education Reform Act 1988 (FEU, 1989) these geographical differences were shown to lead to contrasting and iniquitous provision. In training programmes for employment, the effect of geographical difference is marked. In some rural areas, for example, high levels of local unemployment places trainees with special educational needs in an unfavourable position. Certain regions of severe economic hardship, like the North-East of England, have received substantial funding enabling training providers to offer excellent resources to disabled trainees. Inner-city multi-cultural locations can offer more diverse employment opportunities, but there, black and Asian trainees face social prejudice and discrimination from employers. Combating prejudice is an integral feature of effective empowerment.

THE NATURE OF PREJUDICE

The experience of prejudice for young people within marginalised groups in FE has serious implications for their personal well being, learning encounters, training opportunities and employment prospects. In an analysis of the nature of prejudice Lynch (1987) maintains that it is

a feeling of superiority and aversion, which has the potential to lead to unequal behaviour and therefore injustice and even violence towards persons and groups against whom that prejudice is focussed.

(Lynch, 1987, pp. 33–4)

In a society characterised by gross inequalities, the generation of prejudice has far-reaching consequences for vulnerable individuals or groups. These include emotional, social, material and physical damage and the development of negative self-images. For these students the experience of prejudice entails, for example, low expectations from some college staff, a high level of surveillance and narrow stereotyping.

Recent research (FEU, 1987) indicated that racial prejudice amongst some FE college staff led to low expectations of Asian students, such that their language difficulties were perceived as learning problems. The relationship between prejudice and learning experience was evident:

Some staff revealed disparaging attitudes towards courses which were largely filled by black students. In describing a vocational preparation course which had over three years moved from 20%–30% black intake to 84%, one member of staff referred to the course as having become devalued.

'By having such a large ethnic minority intake the course will be devalued and that will serve to bring about its own downfall.'

(FEU, 1987, p. 31)

This example illustrates a common pattern among professionals in which the emphasis is upon language difficulty as a problem rather than a reflection of cultural diversity and richness. It also reminds us of the pervasive nature of prejudice, in which negative attitudes to devalued groups are perpetuated and reinforced.

We have already indicated that the low demands made on people in day centres can reinforce their special school experience, making them passive dependants, reluctant to display initiative (Barnes, 1990). Expectations of an active social life for young people who experience severe physical disabilities can be markedly different from those of their peers. Prejudice about the nature of disability can lead to society taking an asexual view of their needs. If they do express interest in sexual relationships, it is often anticipated that this should be with other disabled people only. Yet, as Cheaney (1990) reports, disabled people will not necessarily select disabled partners. Prejudice about sexuality is a significant issue:

> Many social workers and parents deny that disabled people have sexual feelings and see no reason to promote such an idea since 'No-one's going to fancy him or her anyway.'
>
> (Cheaney, 1990, p. 45)

Such low expectations of potential relationships can serve to foster passive dependency and stifle initiative in young people who are denied the risk of rejection.

People with learning difficulties are usually subjected to a high level of surveillance, ostensibly for their own safety and the well-being of society. The pressure upon them to conform to a social model of appropriate behaviour can be seen as a facet of societal prejudice. Yet, within this concept of what constitutes 'appropriate' behaviour is a narrow stereotyping of potential capabilities. Students with Down's Syndrome, for example, are rarely considered 'employable'. The fact that they are demonstrably different can distort any comprehension of their individuality, including their varied capabilities (Booth, 1987). Prejudice is about the blinkered way in which we see people. Professional perspectives can vary dramatically from the perceptions of close friends, as the following example illustrates:

> Mr Davis has a mental age of 3 years, 2 months. I.Q. = 18. Severe impairment of adaptive behaviour, severe range of mental retardation.

> Ed likes people and enjoys visiting in the neighbourhood. He loves music, dancing and sweeping. He likes loading

vending machines and operating mechanical equipment.
He likes to go shopping.

(O'Brien and Mount, 1990, p. 6)

It is hard to imagine that these two descriptions are of the same person. One provides little encouragement for positive expectations, whilst the other emphasises particular endearing qualities. What is of serious concern is that the underlying assumptions in the professional perspective could have inhibiting repercussions for this individual's quality of life.

BEING 'NORMAL'

What is 'normal' living for most young people? It is about the rich fabric of life, including an interest in physical appearance, fashion, friendships, sex and social interchanges. The influence of the prevailing model of successful living conveyed by the media can be extremely potent. Young people are portrayed as beautiful, confident and having 'a good time'. In such a context, young people with disabilities and learning difficulties can feel ostracised. This disparity with the popular model of youth culture has to be understood, especially when disabled students are coming into further education at 16, often having experienced nothing but the special school system. They are moving from a sheltered context in which disability is the norm. This transfer into mainstream FE can be traumatic, heightening their awareness of how they are perceived as 'different'.

When an 18 year old who has spina bifida and is in a wheelchair turns to you in the college canteen and says:

'I really fancy that girl, but she won't look at me,'

how do you reply? With peer group pressure to build relationships with attractive partners, where does this place young people who fail to fit this model? One of the dilemmas of integration at this vulnerable teenage stage is that it confronts young people with their difference at a time when the impetus to conform can be overwhelming. This young man is conscious of his difference to the degree that it causes him to be critical of self. In this instance, his anticipation of sexual frustration becomes a further illustration of the emotional and psychological

71

suffering which disabled young people can often experience in interaction with able-bodied peers. This suffering can manifest itself in justifiable distress. However, such behaviours may be interpreted as characteristic of emotional immaturity associated with their disabilities. Expressions of deep-felt anger arising from the experiences of exclusion, far from being the basis of further dehumanisation, should be seen as healthy and appropriate. Even where a disabled young person displays all the qualities of successful social interaction, this is often at the cost of superhuman efforts. This process can be divisive in itself. In gaining inclusion into the able-bodied community, these exceptional individuals may feel compelled to dissociate themselves from identification with their disabled peers. In addressing this issue, Vasey (1990) argues that there are

> strong pressures on us to be 'normal' and to fight on an individual level against the injustices we face, which work against our collective strength.
>
> (Vasey, 1990, p. 75)

Gains at an individual level must never be at the expense of the pursuit of change at a wider socio-economic level.

Building friendships is a very important facet of human development which contributes towards healthy growth. The process of making and sustaining friendships is demanding. For young people with disabilities and learning difficulties, these demands can be particularly complex. If they have attended special schools and continued into special courses in further education, the likelihood is that they have been bussed in from far-flung neighbourhoods. The degree to which they can enjoy informal interchange and participate in college social events is limited by transport restrictions. For many, being bussed for long distances makes for a very long and tiring day. Transport is not the only barrier to establishing relationships. A further difficulty is related to the degree of surveillance which they experience. Superficial acquaintanceships can be fostered within a group. Close friendships need space and privacy. This is a right which is often denied to disabled young people. The paradox, which has to be coped with, is that part of their life skills programme will involve the evaluation of their capacity to develop and sustain friendships. Thus, the institutional context which makes the establishment of friendships difficult requires the formal assessment of these skills.

In a discussion about the needs which friendships meet, Firth and Rapley (1990) suggest that these can be described as

Providing non-judgemental warmth and understanding, or empathy; developing and confirming self-identity; and, raising and sustaining self-esteem.

(Firth and Rapley, 1990, p. 47)

For many young people with disabilities and learning difficulties, building a positive self-identity and sustaining self-esteem is a struggle within a society which marginalises and stereotypes them. The process of creating friendships rather than just acquaintances could help to foster identity and self-esteem yet, with so many difficulties to cope with, this growth of close friendship can remain elusive, thus presenting these young people with a Catch–22 situation.

The struggle for positive self-identity is the war against stereotypes. Stereotypes are offensive, restrictive and painful. They are part of the backdrop against which these young people have to interact. The 'normal' model negates celebration of differences. It makes physical or intellectual difference appear deviant. If people look different, they are expected to have different sensibilities. Their need for love, friendship and social stimulus is perceived as being somehow less than the norm. This superficial judgement is offensive to basic human rights. As Duffy (1990) so powerfully describes in her experience of living with disability:

I have learned slowly that how I feel about my body, my life, is not really very different from how non-disabled people feel about themselves. It's simply that they wear the cloak of normality, a concept which renders me naked.

(Duffy, 1990, p. 75)

Her image offers a wonderfully refreshing redefinition of what constitutes 'normality'. In the classic literature which defines the relationship between 'normal' people and those marginalised by various disabilities and differences, it is these different individuals who are expected to 'cloak' themselves in order to make a calculated impression of appropriate behaviour (Edgerton, 1967; Goffman, 1968). Yet, Duffy perceives the 'normal' as cloaking their individual differences and only the visibly different being truly open and unashamed. It is a challenging image, which is perhaps indicative of changing attitudes to the celebration of difference.

However, society generally seems able to cope with addressing just one oppression at a time. Combining two oppressive experiences confuses the stereotyping and forces separate identities. Jeffrey Tate, the internationally acclaimed conductor who is severely disabled with spina bifida, perceives the positive benefits of experiencing disability, when he says:

> I think I'd be a desperately intolerant person if I weren't disabled. I would be very arrogant. I'm arrogant enough anyway, but it takes the edge off. I mean, I have a great sympathy – not just a liberal sympathy but something deeper – for minorities, for people who are outcasts. And I can stand outside situations, and not feel involved – in a good way, as well as a bad way.
> (Jeffrey Tate, interviewed by Barber, 1990, p. 9)

As someone well known and visibly successful, Tate is able to use both his disability and the fact that he is proud to be gay as a means of challenging stereotypes and promoting tolerance.

For young people who are marginalised through being perceived as socially 'different', stereotyping can significantly limit their choices of employment and community participation. For some young people, this stereotyping is into narrow class, race and gender roles. In some YT workshop provision, despite the attempts of certain schemes to challenge stereotyping and to encourage non-typical choices, working-class girls are still being trained for unskilled factory work in which their roles are clearly defined. Sewing options in YT can focus upon 'looking busily occupied' rather than upon developing a wide range of skills. The expectations of job fulfilment are very low, with implications that this is all that a girl with no academic qualifications, living in an area of high unemployment and few work opportunities, can possibly expect. Asian girls in YT can be similarly restricted. Parental perceptions of their role in the family can influence the extent to which they will have a real choice of employment and independence. For staff in YT, this can leave them with the frustration of knowing that training programmes are used as a bridge between leaving school and going into arranged marriages.

Trainees with Down's Syndrome can be stereotyped into traditional roles. In one YT programme, for example, despite a trainee with Down's Syndrome being able to read and write, to type and cope with a word processor, the notion of encouraging a choice of work placement in an office was perceived as completely unrealistic (Corbett, 1991). It may be the young person's preference but prejudice from employers and other staff make YT trainers fearful of pursuing this possibility. It is easier to send the young person into a work placement in the Social Education Centre, where they will pack plastic spoons into bags all day. It is where they will realistically move on to and it is, therefore, perceived as kinder to prepare them for this reality. Yet, as Duffy (1990) says, 'reality' has to be created anew if damaging and confining stereotypes are to be challenged.

CONCLUSION

In this chapter we raise the problems of defining 'empowerment' and 'successful living' in a community characterised by gross economic inequalities and prejudice. Addressing both issues requires the creation of a new reality. The 'community' itself can be highly oppressive and unjust. At certain stages of history, communities have become remarkably intolerant of minorities. Mann (1939) describes education under the Nazis as a system which promoted prejudice and fostered the oppression of minorities within the community. This is clearly an extreme example but we need to recognise the level of intolerance within our present community if the experiences of minorities are to be understood. The 'reality' which they meet has to be challenged.

Empowerment can come about only if the powerful are prepared to relinquish power. It is not for the isolated individual to claim power. This, in itself, becomes an onerous oppression. The importance of self-help groups and support networks, to promote solidarity for minority groups, cannot be underestimated. As we have already acknowledged, this challenges the 'professional' role. As professionals are often involved in establishing and sustaining 'self-advocacy' groups, they have to learn to face up to their own roles in promoting oppression and they need to recognise just how far they are prepared to cope with the repercussions of real choices. Empowerment, if it is to be effective, will inevitably entail a degree of conflict. This involves professionals and parents having to readjust to a new and often uncomfortable reality. This can promote a painful sense of loss, which has to be addressed. Farrell (1990), in describing the establishment of a women's forum to support women with learning difficulties who were living in the community, recognises the delicacy of real empowerment:

> Time must be set aside for the 'bereavement process'. Workers may find themselves entering a void and feel 'immobilised' by its effects. It is important to realise that out of the void comes new life and this is a very creative and enriching experience. The forum is still learning to 'go with the pace' and to handle bereavement and loss with sensitivity.
>
> (Farrell, 1990, p. 47)

In supporting empowerment, professionals have to move beyond tokenism and surface compartmentalising. All too often, 'speaking for yourselves' is done in one room for two hours on a Friday morning. This system maintains the status quo. To challenge it involves a fundamental and courageous shift of roles. Only through this creative process will new and innovative identities be forged. If tolerance is to be fostered, this will help define the perimeters of what constitutes 'successful' living. One feature which is common to people generally is the need for close friendships. This can define the quality of our living which makes it 'successful' for us as individuals:

It needs to be appreciated that 'relationships' are central to the lives of people with learning difficulties, as for other people. They want people they can go to if they have a problem, people to go places with, people just to be around and to talk to.

(Richardson and Ritchie, 1989, pp. 63–4)

That quality of life which the enrichment of valued social inter-action offers cannot be denied to certain minorities because they have been perceived as 'different'. If 'successful' living is to be reinterpreted to include diverse expressions and needs, this has to involve a complex and difficult struggle. On the one hand, it requires an improved tolerance of differences. On the other, it involves the inclusion of more minority groups within those forums of power and decision-making which have traditionally denied them access. This will inevitably be a protracted and painful process. It can come about only with the active develop-ment of a new concept of 'reality' in relation to both 'community' and 'difference'.

QUESTIONS FOR DISCUSSION

1   We have argued about the centrality of the politics of differ-ence. How far do you agree that this is a significant issue and that our interpretation is valuable?
2   In stereotyping minorities, the community can be a force for oppression. What does 'community' mean in this context and how is change possible?
3   Within a market economy and enterprise culture, how do you understand the meaning of 'successful' living for dis-abled young people?

6

EQUAL OPPORTUNITIES

One of the characteristics of further education is that it offers opportunities and choices which might previously have been denied. It has traditionally been seen as providing a second chance for learning and of opening access. Yet, Whittaker (1991) argues that, for students with learning difficulties:

> Further education is in danger of perpetuating all the negative aspects of segregated provision. It is in danger of failing to respond creatively to individual potential and failing to promote or acknowledge the value of equal challenge where individuals progress in relation to their own efforts and strengths, not some arbitrary notion of normal.
>
> (Whittaker, 1991, p. 24)

In addressing these issues, he illustrates the importance of including special educational within an equal opportunities policy. He identifies both the absolute necessity of such an inclusion and its inevitable complexity. His emphasis also indicates that both the impetus for such policies and their effectiveness involves fundamental values and a capacity for change.

In this chapter, we will explore three related themes which emerge from this context. These can be expressed through the following questions:

- Why should responding to special educational needs be an integral part of an equal opportunities policy?

- Whose values should determine the priorities of such a policy?
- How can we create and effectively implant such policies?

SPECIAL NEEDS AND EQUAL OPPORTUNITIES

In an ideal world, there would be no need for equal opportunities policies. Their very existence reflects a recognition of fundamental problems relating to the distribution of opportunities and privileges in society. For too long, special education has remained apolitical. This means that the focus has been on individual needs to the serious neglect of institutional inertia, structural inequalities and limited access. In further education, this has often meant that staff responsible for special needs are ill-equipped to participate in a political forum.

To merely posit at an individual level remains a limited and naive model for change. Responding to special needs in further education has to challenge systems and structures, including fundamental issues of power and control. This has to involve the special educational needs of students being addressed as a whole-college equal opportunities issue. This depersonalises what are essentially political judgements, involving rights and not needs. However, such an approach can be alien to staff accustomed to working within a narrow focus on individual need, isolated from wider political involvement. Unwittingly, staff in this position can further segregate themselves and their students:

> Somewhat ironically, given the origins of FE special needs provision, special needs staff were on occasion criticised for their isolationism. They tended 'to keep themselves to themselves' and 'to think they are the only ones who can teach special needs students'. While they publicly espoused the principle of integration, some of them seemed privately to prefer 'to protect their students from the big wide world'.
>
> (FEU, 1990, p. 3)

Furthermore, some staff responsible for special needs have argued for a separate special needs policy rather than an inclusion in an equal opportunities policy. They have indicated that this level of exclusion protects the interests of their students. Such an attitude may have arisen from a sceptical caution regarding the often 'bolt-on', tokenistic gesture of including special needs in equal opportunities policies.

We argue that special educational needs must be an integral part of an equal opportunities policy. We argue this on the following grounds:

1 that the issues are complex and contentious, requiring an engagement in power struggles
2 that concepts of 'autonomy', 'choice' and 'empowerment' have to be understood in a structural context
3 that it can offer collective solidarity to marginalised groups, weakened by their isolationism
4 that it can avoid a blinkered approach to meeting individual learner needs by highlighting contradictions within systems and processes.

Edwards (1991) argues that:

> We create practices which reflect and engender notions of individual equality of opportunity. While this provides a pyramid of opportunity for the individuals who are able to compete within the educational market place, it condemns us all to structural relations of power which reproduce inequality. Individuals escape, but structures of inequality and the subordination of groups continues. Unequal opportunity is perpetuated and legitimised within an ideology of equality of opportunity and individual escape rather than social emancipation is the learning project.
>
> (Edwards, 1991, p. 91)

Within his scenario, people with special needs are particularly vulnerable. They are rarely 'individuals who are able to compete within the educational market place' and are, therefore, unlikely to 'escape' but continue to be among the most consistently subordinated of groups.

Placing special needs within an equal opportunities context underscores the real sufferings which result from discrimination. It also legitimises our contention that special needs provision is a political issue. In taking this stance, we are not denying the difficulties experienced by individuals. As we illustrated in our examples of students' perceptions, these are significant problems requiring sensitive support. Disabled authors such as Rieser (1990) and Morris (1990) vividly demonstrate that empowerment develops only from a personal struggle against pain and discrimination allied to the strength which collective support can offer. Ultimately, concerns for empowerment or the enrichment of individual opportunities are rooted in a deeper commitment to the realisation of a just and equitable society.

Addressing special educational needs as an equal opportunities issue involves commitment to secure and consistent funding, to participation within the higher levels of management and to curricular flexibility and responsiveness. Funding is essential for the establishment and maintenance of appropriate and innovative course provision. Unless this fundamental security of resourcing is in situ, special needs provision in further education remains a peripheral area which is devalued and under-resourced. A recent HMI Report (DES, 1991b) highlighted the fragility of funding in this area:

> In some colleges, the complexity of unit costing made it impossible to deduce the criteria for funding link courses. For example, there was much variation from one year to the next, with college management viring funding both away from and to special needs work. In one instance, virement away from special needs had the result that students who had formerly been integrated into a range of mainstream provision were withdrawn and put together, to their disadvantage, on a discrete course.
>
> (DES, 1991b, p. 10)

The issue at stake, in such an example, supports our commitment to rights and not charity. Provision for special needs evolved in further education upon a charitable basis. It reflected a societal attitude towards dependent persons whose level of productivity makes them objects of charity. This deficiency model is replicated in Further Education where special needs has traditionally been under-funded, ill-resourced and reliant upon the goodwill of lecturers with an interest in the area. As the HMI Report highlights, special schools are increasingly involved in fund raising for their effective maintenance. This perpetuates a charitable status. It also allows for professional judgements, like the transferring of students from integrated provision into a discrete course, without consultation with the individuals concerned or their representatives. This most subordinate of groups remains highly vulnerable to decisions of this nature.

The establishment of equal opportunities policies provides the means of raising questions about decision-making within an institution. This implies that the infringement of policy, at whatever level, should legitimately be challenged. Senior management have to share responsibility. At Kingsway College in Camden, for example, the woman Vice Principal has responsibility for equal opportunities, liaising directly with staff co-ordinating multi-ethnic education and disability issues (O'Grady, 1990). Not only does this ensure managerial power to influence staff development and to promote new initiatives, but also it encourages the adoption of an equal opportunities approach to curricular development at all levels. This includes promoting positive images of disability and increasing opportunities for integrated course provision. Through the sustained impact of managerial support a whole-college commitment and shared responsibility can be developed. This is not to deny that difficult decisions will have to be made, nor that tensions will arise through contradictory pressures. However, those decisions will be made within a context of dialogue and consultation.

One of the advantages of setting special needs in an equal opportunities context is that it gives centrality to 'curricula for all' issues. This challenges notions of exclusion and possibilities of complacency. Instead of marginalising certain groups and their perspectives, it both acknowledges the importance of difference and reflects diversity within curricular provision. An example of such an approach is offered by Van Dyke (1990) who asks:

> Are the contributions that women, black, disabled, working class or lesbian and gay academics, researchers or writers have made to the discipline included in your course or are they ignored or marginalised?
>
> (Van Dyke, 1990, p. 11)

Taking this stance ensures that the perspectives of disabled people are valued and given significance, with long-term implications for the self-esteem of disabled students.

In addition to addressing the content of the curriculum, the status of the curriculum available for many students with special needs has to be changed. As we have illustrated, the last decade has seen a succession of special curricular frameworks brought into FE. Whilst these were necessary stages in ensuring that students with learning difficulties were included, they were not offering equality of status for these students. Their curriculum framework provided a special programme which offered no progression into mainstream provision but maintained a separate and, by definition, inferior status. As Wardman (1990) suggests, the gap between policy and practice is often a negation of equality within the institution. She says, of the college in which she worked:

> There is a dearth of the vocational type of course which is far more appropriate for those with Moderate Learning Difficulties, Severe Learning Difficulties and students with a Hearing Impairment. This also limits progression. There is at present no course for the 'FURTHER ON' student to move on to after their course is completed. 'FURTHER ON' is a course for students with Severe Learning Difficulties, aged 16–20. The majority of students go into open employment, but in recent years only one has progressed onto another course within the College, and that was another Special Educational Needs Course for students with Moderate Learning Difficulties, not a mainstream course. And yet, the policy states:
>
> 'In providing specially designed courses for students with learning difficulties and/or disabilities, College is offering bridges into the mainstream curriculum. College will continue to review aims and objectives of specially designed courses to ensure that they continue to meet the needs of students with Special Educational Needs, and to promote maximum integration and progression'.
>
> (Wardman, 1990, p. 34)

Wardman's reflections indicate that the requests made in *A*

'Special' Professionalism (DES, 1987), for a flexible range of provision which offers an opportunity for progression, have not yet been widely addressed.

From our perspective, it would be misleading to interpret this to imply that all students can attend all courses. This is not equality of opportunity. What we are suggesting is that students with special educational needs are entitled to a curriculum which offers them progression into a range of choices. They are also entitled to a curriculum which offers them certification. Until now, special courses in FE, and special programmes in YT, have rarely provided any form of qualification. The introduction of National Vocational Qualifications (NVQs) has the potential to remedy this situation.

NVQs are competence-based measures of the ability to do a job. In theory, they are changing the curriculum by adopting open and flexible learning and providing support services, improved access and facilities to assess prior learning (INSIGHT, 1991). In practice, however, Unwin (1990) cautions that they may place unrealistic pressure upon some students which simply reinforces their experience of failure. The capacity for providers to be sufficiently flexible when faced with external criteria from bodies such as the TECs is restricted. The key measure within FE and training is on 'employability'. This indicates a specific set of values, which are reflected in the new government White Paper (DES, 1991a). We would wish to challenge priorities becoming exclusively determined by such values.

RESOURCING FOR EQUALITY OF VALUE

As Hutchinson and Tennyson (1986) recognised and a recent OECD (1991) survey confirmed, if young people with disabilities are going to have equality of opportunity they must receive appropriate continuity of support. This requires significant resource commitments for service providers. Molloy (1991) illustrates the example of a disabled student who was ultimately able to attend a mainstream FE college, but only by being provided with special transport, specific communication aids, physiotherapy and personal support. This complex arrangement is expensive. FE colleges are being encouraged 'to make it easier for people to progress quickly to occupationally specific qualifications' (DES, 1991a, p. 18). Whilst this is related to the notion of raising training standards, it does ignore the non-vocational element of further education. For the disabled student to whom Molloy refers, employment opportunities might be limited. He will also be very costly to support. Does this make his inclusion non-viable? One of the ironies of this situation is that, whilst official ideology legitimising such changes claims to widen access and extend choice, the vulnerability of marginalised groups becomes even more acute. As we have already illustrated, there are indications that training programmes for the most disadvantaged are becoming the victims of 'rationalisation' by the TECs (Ainley, 1990). Coupled with this are serious threats to cut back adult education provision, limiting further the opportunities for progression.

The reality of most current provision in FE colleges is that of inaccessible buildings and ill-resourced, low-status special needs departments. The struggle for change, therefore, will be extremely difficult. It requires a reassessment of priorities, an allocation of adequate resources and fundamental shifts in values. Thus, the creation of equal opportunities policies entails for the participants an engagement with conflicts of interest and interpretation. This is a central part of the process which leads to 'the initiation and management of change' (DES, 1987, p. 11) which has to involve college management in order to forge whole-college policies.

If the status of special needs is to be raised in FE, it has to become a whole-college responsibility and not delegated to a 'caring' section of the institution. There are many instances in which students with disabilities and learning difficulties have been placed in a 'Community Care' or 'Health' section, alongside predominantly female staff and students (e.g. Corbett, 1987; Turnham, 1991). This assumption that it is only the 'caring' section of the college which can accommodate special needs is oppressive both to disabled students and to women. For the disabled students, it constricts their integration into the broader college community. For the female staff and students, it equates training for caring professions with taking an unequal share of what should be a whole-college responsibility. Such delegation to a 'caring' section negates equality of opportunity as it reinforces stereotypes: the stereotype of the dependent disabled student and the stereotype of the caring female.

Yet, this prevalent pattern illustrates a dilemma in creating equality of opportunities. For disabled students coming into mainstream FE from special schools, their experience can be confusing, sometimes frightening and possibly lonely. A 'Caring' section, which includes a special needs base room, can be a considerable source of comfort and security. Whilst students may seek such support, these practices can be restrictive and debilitating, inhibiting personal growth and risk-taking.

Providing equality of opportunity requires a respect for differences within a supportive environment. The oppression of disabled people is variously experienced. Within the FE context, it can take the form of an unadaptive physical environment, a traditionally 'macho' culture and a narrow vocational course structure, all of which contribute to their alienation. This does not just apply to disabled students. The *few* disabled lecturers who are included in mainstream FE are, themselves, the subjects of hostilities. Morris (1987), herself a disabled lecturer, reflected that even in a college which prides itself on a policy of equal opportunities, feelings of prejudice exist among colleagues:

> being treated as an equal is very much on the surface. Scratch this surface and you find the fear and contempt which underlies much of the discrimination against people who don't measure up to what we consider to be 'normal'.
> (Morris, 1987, p. 262)

This evaluation illustrates the complexity of the issues which need to be addressed, particularly those of underlying attitudes.

Taking Morris's perspective, we need critically to evaluate what measuring up to 'normality' means in a mainstream FE context. A 'normal' FE ethos might involve covert discrimination on the grounds of class, race, sex and disability. Traditionally, white male values have dominated the structure of mainstream further education. Part of the new development of community colleges has been to redress the balance. Creating different priorities has involved placing high value on previously neglected groups. The John Wheatley College, for example, which opened in August 1989 in the East End of Glasgow is committed to meeting the needs of vastly different communities. As well as including the traditionally vocational FE students from the more prosperous areas of the city, the college is responding to the needs of people in Easterhouse, an area of high unemployment, poor housing, ill-health, drug abuse and truancy. It is now attracting into college students who have failed at school, experienced learning difficulties and who are returning to education after a number of years. Such an emphasis is clearly time-consuming, expensive and contentious. If students who have already failed in formal education are being effectively nurtured into FE, there will be no guarantee that they can meet the increasingly taxing demands which match employers' expectations (DES, 1991a). Placing high value on low status groups presents managers with conflicting measures of what constitutes success.

Our argument is that equal opportunities cannot be addressed within a single dimension like 'disability' or 'race'. It is necessary to consider the interrelationship between age, gender, race, class and disability. Compartmentalising these issues is counter-productive to the realisation of effective change.

IMPLEMENTING EFFECTIVE POLICY

Making equal opportunities policies work must be the concern of *all* personnel within the institution. Thus the policy should apply not only to lecturers but also to all staff. Addressing specific issues like disability or race should not be the sole responsibility of specialist staff. For example, Harries (1990), a special needs co-ordinator in a college, illustrates the practical application of such an approach in relation to catering staff and their views of, and interactions with, people with learning difficulties. Among the points she makes are the following:

- Speak to them as adults and not children.
- Treat them as adults.
- Refer to them as 'adults/students' and not 'children'.
- Expect adult behaviour.
- Please do not use expressions like 'cripple' or 'spastic' as they are very insulting and degrading.
- Don't give free or extra portions of food. We want the students to be responsible for themselves and their own money.
- Please do not offer food, but rather wait for the student to indicate what they want.

(Harries, 1990, pp. 42–3)

These illustrations confirm our contention that combating discrimination is not *solely* about confronting hostilities. It also involves challenging inappropriate kindness. The implementation of policy has to permeate all facets of institutional life including staff/student interactions, the organisation of the college, teaching styles and expectations, curriculum content and staff development.

Careful consideration must be given to the creation and maintenance of an effective infrastructure to implement policy. Fundamental features will be: the inclusion of monitoring and evaluation; the allocation of co-ordinating roles; clear channels of communication; and definite outcomes. The extent to which any policy will be given credence depends upon demonstrations of commitment from management and within departmental structures. If staff throughout the college are to be encouraged to exert more concerted effort to implement this policy, they will require effective role models. Senior members of management have to display commitment in their daily practice. Aspects of policy will need to be revised regularly in response to the impact of institutional change and external influences. The pressures of interpersonal conflicts within the college and of external demands from employers and funding bodies can threaten fundamental values.

It would be a mistake to assume that FE colleges offer a homogeneous entity. As Nelson (1991) stresses in his study of South Manchester Community College, the reality of the community of a further education college is that it represents a diverse range of cultures and structures according to the dominant activities within the departments. Such a mixture of separate cultures has to be addressed. The 'macho' culture of a traditional Building Department, for example, might be particularly insensitive and unresponsive to concerning itself with issues of race, gender and disability. If we are effectively to implement an equal opportunities policy, therefore, the differences between departments have to be acknowledged and strategies adapted accordingly.

Implementing an equal opportunities policy is not a one-off activity. People will be at various stages of development and experience. It has to be a perennial concern, reflecting a long-term vision. Policies need to be refined, changed or supplemented in the light of reflection or developments. Well-designed, systematic and appropriately resourced staff training, as Cooper (1988) emphasises in relation to special needs, has to be introduced and maintained through a process of networking. For low-status lecturers in FE, who are struggling from a restricted power base, this continuity of support is vital. As we have already recognised, special needs co-ordinators usually have limited power within the FE hierarchy, whilst ironically, they are concerned with student empowerment.

SPECIAL NEEDS AND EQUAL OPPORTUNITIES

A pattern has developed in many colleges in which a separate policy for special needs has been introduced alongside an equal opportunities policy. In our current research, we are finding that some special needs co-ordinators have already established the special needs policy and are then asked to help develop an equal opportunities policy. One co-ordinator reflected that

> this Borough is very much behind the times. I've had it said to me by somebody very high up in college, when asked what they felt the future developments were for special needs in the college, 'Well, we only have 2% ethnic minority in this Borough, so we haven't got a problem.' They didn't actually address the whole issue of people with learning difficulties. People with physical disabilities just didn't even seem to enter the equation.
>
> (Interview, June 1991)

This example indicates why some practitioners supporting students with special needs in FE are cautious about allowing a special needs policy to become absorbed within equal opportunities policies. They fear that in a superficial inclusion real needs may be overlooked.

In some instances, the special needs policy which staff have developed is such that it is emulated as good practice. This co-ordinator found that

> What has actually come about is that, instead of us in special needs feeling that we are behind everybody else, the good practice that we have in equal opportunities, in

89

terms of the individual curriculum, is showing other people they have a lot of catching up to do.

(Interview, July, 1991)

Whilst this co-ordinator was reflecting a move within his college to set special needs within a whole-college commitment to equal opportunities, another co-ordinator regretted that her staff were often unsupported:

my worry about the special needs section is that it is a very dedicated, very committed group of people, but we're far too insular; we are doing it all ourselves. That lets everybody else off the hook.

(Interview, June, 1991)

These varied responses to the implementation of policy demonstrate the different experiences of practitioners. For some special needs co-ordinators, their involvement in changing policy and practice through the college is significant. For others, it is peripheral.

In the following chapter, we will examine the perspectives and experiences of a range of special needs co-ordinators, working in a variety of contexts. Their complex and constantly changing role offers another dimension of the struggle for choice.

QUESTIONS FOR DISCUSSION

1 What do you understand by 'equal opportunities' and how would you describe the key components?
2 We have argued that a focus upon single issues ignores the complexity of 'equal opportunities'. To what extent to you agree?
3 What part do you see management playing in the creation and maintenance of policies? What strategies should be used to involve them?

7

CO-ORDINATORS IN A PROCESS OF CHANGE

In 'setting the scene' in Chapter 1 we argued that the special needs area had largely developed in further education on a charitable basis. This resulted in initial courses which were unstructured, under-staffed and ill-resourced. Generally, special needs co-ordinators were brought in from the special school sector and were unfamiliar with the politics of FE. The implication of such an emphasis was that much practice in this field was reliant upon goodwill and that the curriculum and objectives for these students was given inadequate consideration. Subsequently, expectations and demands were often low and opportunities for progression minimal.

The current role of special needs co-ordinators has to be understood within this context. Factors influencing them are both historical and political. The way in which 'special needs' was conceived within their institution, its geographical and economic location and its prevailing ethos will all determine how they are able to play their roles. Current changes within a market-led economy are requiring them to become more adaptable and display increasing versatility. The role of the co-ordinator has become distinctive in relation to other participants in FE. Whilst, on the whole, subject specialists work within clearly defined boundaries, the special needs co-ordinator has a liaison role which combines a mounting range of responsibilities. This liaison role can give co-ordinators access to arenas which other lecturers of similar status are denied. Such participation combines both enriching and frustrating aspects.

One of us (Corbett, 1987) has experienced the diversity of this role and her experience reflects that of other co-ordinators interviewed in our current research. Although commanding only low status in the college hierarchy, she had access to committees at which all other participants were heads of departments, to headteachers and managers of centres and to the Vice Principal as the manager with responsibility for special needs. The frustration of such liaison was that her power was restricted and, thus, changes had to come about through coercion and diplomacy. The value was that it offered a rich opportunity to learn how to cope with the politics of discourse through entry into a range of forums. One of the key lessons learnt from this experience was that becoming respected and valued by different groups, including college managers and caretakers, was essential for the promotion of those students whose needs were being represented. If the co-ordinator is widely accepted, this facilitates the increased integration of the students concerned.

PLAYING A CENTRAL ROLE

The part which the co-ordinator plays is central to both institutional and community participation for students with disabilities or learning difficulties. There are two key aspects to this role. The first one is that of providing continuity of support. Kjellen (1991) describes the benefits of the inclusive role played by the Kurator in Denmark, who has responsibility for ensuring that young people with disabilities and learning difficulties continue to receive the support services they need through compulsory schooling, into further education, community activities and employment. Whilst we have no comparable system in Britain, there are aspects of the Kurator's role which the special needs co-ordinator fulfils. He or she has to liaise with local schools, parents and employers. The services of therapists, psychologists and social workers are often negotiated through the co-ordinator.

The second key aspect of the co-ordinator's role is that of internal, institutional networking. This includes working alongside welfare staff and, as Harries (1990) noted, liaising with catering and caretaking staff. This networking involves: negotiating access to buildings; demanding adequate material resources and staffing; developing the curriculum; devising and monitoring policy.

Support for special needs co-ordinators can come from various external sources. The special needs advisory service is one.

Another is the Inspectorate, which has made a significant contribution to the special needs area in FE (e.g. DES, 1988) and has offered valuable support. Recognising the low power base of most co-ordinators, HMI have acted as advocates on their behalf to present critical demands to management (DES, 1987). Skill: The National Bureau for Students with Disabilities has campaigned for students whilst providing a continued and substantial support for their lecturers. In some INSET provision (Blake and Blake, 1988), co-ordinators worked together to prepare materials for staff development in their respective colleges, thus offering material support and stimulus.

The centrality of the co-ordinator's role to their students' experiences is evident. What also distinguishes them from other comparable staff in FE is the level of commitment expected of them. For example, while other members of staff might go off the premises in their lunch-hour, the co-ordinator will often have to stay in their base room, where students can have access to them in any emergency and where they can be available to cope with the many daily problems which arise.

DIVERSITY AND DILEMMAS

Like all other participants in FE, college special needs co-ordinators are being influenced by current changes which have come about since the Education Act 1988 and the subsequent White Paper. Among these influences are the following: promoting the institutional image; becoming increasingly cost-effective; appealing to many diverse markets; extending choices and influences; being dominated by the employer-led influence of the TEC; engaged in inter-college competition.

Such diversity has led to a more complex and entrepreneurial role for special needs co-ordinators and, for some, a new status as managers. The impetus for change, as identified in the new White Paper, both legitimises the market model in relation to education and emphasises the issue of outcomes. To some extent, this new emphasis is shifting the focus of the special needs co-ordinator's commitment.

In our current research, we are finding that the influence of the TECs is permeating special needs provision. This co-ordinator, for example, said that

I have already made successful application to the TECs for the funding of two projects within the next 18 months to, possibly, the value of £80,000.

(Interview, June 1991)

These successful applications were out of six originally submitted. Whilst this has brought substantial funding into the special needs area, it has required considerable preparation, administration and external liaison. As this same co-ordinator goes on to say:

The management are happy for me to come away from the contact of the chalk face.... for example, last year we had, from school leavers, seventeen and a half thousand student hours within the college, paid for by TVEI. Well, of course, if I can do anything like that it justifies me being away. That's the kind of changes that are coming in.

(Interview, June, 1991)

This example, which has been replicated in many of our interviews, reflects the entrepreneurial spirit influencing the role of co-ordinators.

Such activities may well be seen as essential, both by the management of the college as well as by the co-ordinator, although some of the reasons for this involvement will differ. However, engaging in this form of enterprise culture will have its price. Co-ordinators will be faced with a series of possible dilemmas. For example, appealing to many diverse markets may detract from providing continuity of support for students. Producing submissions for funding, writing reports for external and internal evaluations, engaging in increasing committee work and establishing and maintaining contacts with outside agencies all absorbs time, thought and energy. This is becoming more acute as being successful in such activities is increasingly perceived as an indicator of effective professional practice. Within this context, the need to maintain acceptable relationships and lines of communication with both staff and students will become a point of tension for the co-ordinator.

This may be experienced as a continual difficulty due to the cumulative impact of such pressures or, more severely, at particular moments when specific dilemmas arise.

Whilst, to a degree, all lecturers in FE are mediators of contradictory pressures, the position of the co-ordinators is particularly delicate. They have a central role to play in relation to the power structures within the institution. Their struggle is against marginalisation. If they are to empower both themselves and their students, they need to share responsibility with colleagues. However, they are often disempowered by the system in which they work. In addition, they have to engage in constant self-criticism. The legacy of a special, discrete provision, often isolated in a 'caring' department, is one which they need to challenge. A fundamental aspect of their effectiveness will be related to the degree to which such critical reflections lead to actions for change. Meeting the pragmatics of the moment whilst having a clear vision and commitment to wider objectives is the challenge for the co-ordinator.

As Hammond and Collins (1991) emphasise, the importance is to

'think globally, but act locally', which is far preferable to either of the other extremes: either becoming so overwhelmed by macro-level problems that you become paralysed into empty theorising; or ignoring macro-level problems and 'doing something practical', without realising that you will probably reproduce existing injustices in your own work. Have you managed to find a balance between these two extremes in your life and work?

(Hammond and Collins, 1991, p. 83)

Meeting the demands of the market place presents co-ordinators with a perennial dilemma, in which they have to balance their accountability to the institution with their commitment to student entitlement and their own development as reflective practitioners.

CURRICULUM ISSUES

The special needs co-ordinator has a responsibility to develop the curriculum at two levels: within discrete course provision and in mainstream learning support. Developing the special curriculum is an aspect of the co-ordinator's role which they inherited by default. When students with learning difficulties came in to further education, there was no suitable provision for them. This left co-ordinators, without guidance or resources, to 'put together' the special curriculum in FE. *From Coping to Confidence* (Bradley, 1985) was, to a considerable extent, an early attempt to respond to the evident needs of ill-supported co-ordinators. This involvement in developing the curriculum within special courses is still an important element of the role for most co-ordinators.

Whilst developing a careful structured framework was essential, it has caused dilemmas for the co-ordinator. Many special courses for students with severe learning difficulties purport to follow the principles of 'normalisation'. However, as Turnham (1991) notes in her role as a special needs lecturer, defining what is 'age-appropriate' can conflict with prevailing fashions:

> This mechanism ended in total failure when, after lengthy and various attempts to persuade several female life preparation students to give up wearing white ankle socks in favour of tights, short socks, mostly white, suddenly became very fashionable and seemed to adorn every other pair of ankles in the building.
>
> (Turnham, 1991, p. 231)

Whilst there is humour in an example like this, there are serious implications in any attempt to constrain choice. Special needs tutors undoubtedly have more power over their students than conventional FE lecturers. Within this relationship, attempts to promote 'empowerment' are restrained by pragmatism and concern. Brown and Smith (1989), in an analogy between the women's movement and the disability movement, argue that 'service users are caught up in a vicious circle whereby their deviation from this supported norm deprives them of personal power and authenticity' (p. 109). For the FE support staff themselves, their real concern may be that, in offering choice, students may place themselves at risk or follow directions which could lead to a deteriorating quality of life. In the instance of a student with severe cerebral palsy, for example, who had originally been given physiotherapy as part of the curriculum, 'empowerment' could make this student select alternative priorities with possible implications for their physical well-being. In the struggle for choice, the opportunity to take risks presents both parties with serious dilemmas. The extent to which staff can engage together in careful and critical discussion of their work becomes a crucial issue. They have to address diversity of need whilst, at the same time, working towards equality of opportunity.

A constant difficulty facing the special needs co-ordinator is being able to evaluate the purpose of the special curriculum and the opportunities it offers for progression. There are instances where students with learning difficulties move from one special course to another, either within a single institution or across institutions. Attending a special course can become an end in itself because there are no alternatives. It is part of the cycle of inequalities which vulnerable people experience. This cycle includes the variables of geographical location and, currently, LEA policies. One co-ordinator we interviewed captures the frustrations within this position:

> For people with post–19 moderate learning difficulties, it's very much seen as a last opportunity, in that there are people who've already done one or two courses . . . some people are on their fourth college course by the time they reach that post–19 course.
>
> (SEN Co-ordinator interviewed July 1991)

The knowledge that there is nothing at the end of it is the issue. To address this dilemma, there needs to be an inclusion of a preparation for the difficulties and frustrations which are likely to arise in the future. Fenton and Hughes (1989) recognised this and presented it as an integral component of supporting student empowerment.

Such an intractable situation does challenge the purpose of these courses. The extent to which this becomes ambiguous or cynical can lead to a disabling effect on expectations. Co-ordinators can be driven into offering students enrolment on to yet another special course because it is a safety net to prevent their falling into stagnation at home. The issue of 'curriculum entitlement' becomes lost in this scenario. It can become a curriculum for containment with associated low expectations. As Warnock (1991) reflects on developments in integration since the late 1970s:

The safety net, whatever form it takes, is no substitute for entitlement to education. Neither is the concept of 'caring'. The disabled and disadvantaged do not need 'care', they need education on a basis of *equal rights*.

(Warnock, 1991, p. 151)

To effect this education on the basis of equal rights, part of the co-ordinator's current role is to create opportunities to access the mainstream curriculum.

Our current research into the role of the special needs co-ordinator has made us aware that most of those we interviewed felt that support for learning in the mainstream curriculum was now a key area of development. In order to promote this across the college, it is essential that they develop managerial skills and gain general credibility. This is being developed in various ways within different contexts. One co-ordinator, for example, says:

I took on the role of the college staff development officer which actually gives me some remission from teaching time but also gets you seen as somebody who is involved in curriculum matters and that you can actually talk about other things as well. That has been hard work but I think that is a really important step, giving credibility to the whole of the special needs area.

(Interview, November 1991)

This co-ordinator also encouraged her special needs staff team to become members of a range of committees and working parties.

The co-ordinator's responsibility is increasingly extending beyond supporting discrete courses to an overall provision of learning support structures. However, we would contend and those we have interviewed demonstrate that this involves more than the creation and adoption of learning support packages. Resource materials of this nature are a necessary part of changing practice. Yet, they are not, in and of themselves, a sufficient condition to effect more general change in policy and teaching objectives within the institution. This develops only from status being given to supporting all learners. 'Special needs' can no longer be seen as a marginalised provision. As a co-ordinator said of his curriculum development:

I'm not prepared any more to water down what I offer students because it's special needs and we don't want to rock the boat and we've got to be very careful. My attitude is that if you want a quality provision then you have to pay for it.

(Interview, October 1991)

He has promoted a 'quality provision' by creating departmental co-ordinators throughout the college, who share ownership of the curriculum for students who need learning support. Instead of the generally unsatisfactory situation which often developed in colleges, where special needs tutors were expected to adapt subject areas beyond their experience, here the subject tutors adapt their own material. Consequently, within their modifications, a vocational curriculum of real quality and relevance can be fostered. This type of curriculum development is that which is most likely to lead to national qualifications.

FACILITATORS AND DEVELOPERS

This progression to becoming what one co-ordinator described as 'a facilitator and a developer' requires an erosion of specialist mystique. This includes a delegation of responsibility. There has always been an ambiguity surrounding the role of special needs co-ordinators. In its most extreme form it can entail the combination of being in a peripheral position with being expected to provide detailed knowledge and solutions on every aspect of special needs. The label 'special needs expert' has historically contributed to their separateness from an engagement in broader cross-college issues. A more public participation has, on the one hand, the benefit of challenging previous suspicions, confusion and misinformation and, on the other hand, provides fresh ideas, insights and contributions to a shared curriculum development. If this development is to progress successfully it has to involve a struggle to learn new strategies, skills and perceptions. We have no illusions about the complexity and discomfort of the task. It necessitates a persistent commitment to a vision of the future which entails change.

At a time when FE practitioners are being bombarded with pressures to change it might seem callous to be advocating an alternative support service which involves them in increased responsibility. Therefore, giving staff periods of non-teaching time in which to create effective learning support materials is essential. Reliance on goodwill, a legacy of the special needs provision in FE, is no longer acceptable. The micro-politics of college life involves a struggle over competing objectives, arising from external pressures and institutional constraints. Working within such a context demands a vital learning process. This includes a willingness to listen, sensitivity, political astuteness and the ability to seize on unanticipated opportunities. No real change comes easily. Where that change is also threatening the status quo, it entails conflict and commitment.

In our book, which is concerned with student rights and choices, a consideration of the co-ordinator's role has been, not incidental, but essential. They are the gatekeepers to real opportunities at many levels. The effectiveness of their efforts will be instrumental in providing a quality experience for the students they represent. In this respect, the perennial question they need to address is, 'Whose side are we on?' Theirs is a moral dilemma. To what extent should they engage, as Cassara (1990) suggests, in supporting their students in disability politics by challenging the system? Should they prioritise their efforts in working closely with mainstream colleagues to create an inclusive curriculum? Or, has theirs become a purely managerial post of political tactics and negotiation? These competing demands can actually lead to diminished job satisfaction. As one co-ordinator said:

> I find that the things that I like doing I get to do less and less of because of other pressures.
> (Interview, November 1991)

Increased managerial responsibilities pose serious difficulties for co-ordinators. Their required involvement in other arenas within the college reduces the time they can give to talking with students and, thereby, understanding their perceptions. They then run the risk of a reliance upon second-hand experience offered by colleagues. Their skills outside the college, specifically in 'tuning-in' to the TECs which have come to assume a powerful influence in education and training, can transform them into business partners rather than educationists. As Fennell (1991) demonstrates, college principals measure performance on successful collaboration with the TECs. The co-ordinator has to be seen to perform with business acumen.

CONCLUSION

The special needs co-ordinator's role has developed through several stages in the last decade. Originally adopting a special education model, it involved a focus on individual needs and a specialised curriculum. For some co-ordinators, the restrictions of their college context have kept them predominantly within this stage. Others have moved into the development of a learning support structure across the college. This stage might be termed 'shared responsibility'. In seeking to realise an inclusively participatory environment for all students and staff, the role of the co-ordinator can be seen as a means to an end and not an end in itself. This is vividly captured in this co-ordinator's comment that

> until we are at a stage where we no longer need to chip away at people's awareness and raise those issues time and again, you'll need someone to protect those students' interests. But, if we are really working towards a hard college approach there has to be a time when we say 'Well, actually, do we need that person?'
>
> (Interview, September 1991)

This reflection entails the vision of a way ahead, the recognition of those difficulties involved and the ultimate dissolution of the co-ordinator's role. Such an approach is 'hard' in a variety of respects. 'Special needs', if made a part of whole-college provision, will become just one aspect of quality assurance. As such, it will be what all staff are expected to address within their commitment to curriculum entitlement: a 'hard' approach in which they cannot abdicate responsibilities. Creating this transformation involves the dismantling of special needs empires in FE. This is the 'hard' cost of real inclusion.

QUESTIONS

1 What kind of staff development do co-ordinators need if they are to become effective 'facilitators and developers'?

101

2 What do you see as the main tensions within the tasks the co-ordinator undertakes?
3 How far do you agree with our conclusion that the co-ordinator's role must be a means to an end rather than an end in itself?

CONCLUSION

The changing emphasis within the co-ordinator's role reflects our focus in this book. For the co-ordinators, it has involved a shift from an individualised model of special need to supporting a whole college approach. Our intention has been to move out from an individualised notion of special needs in FE to contextualise it in a wider and more complex setting. For the co-ordinators, their changing role has involved them in struggle in the institution. For us, the notion of struggle for change is central to the book.

We introduced this book by discussing some of the major changes being imposed on further education by government. Further changes in the funding of institutions, in the curricula and assessment processes have yet to work themselves through the system. However, even at this stage, it is clear that recognising the rights of students with special educational needs is not a priority. Whilst there may be benefits to be derived from the current changes, they do not reflect a coherent plan. Thus, the legacy of a piecemeal, weakly planned and poorly co-ordinated 'policy' is in danger of being repeated. We wish to advocate, as an imperative, the introduction of a national policy on post-school provision which has both the political will and resource support underpinning it. This demand for legislation, in which the rights of disabled people are enshrined, is vital if 'choice' is to be more than rhetoric. At all stages of the development, disabled people and their organisations or advocates should be fully represented in the processes of planning, deliberation and consultation leading up to legislation. A reliance on market forces is no substitute for responsible government action.

It would be negligent, on our part, not to raise the question of management responsibility with regard to the development and maintenance of good practice for all students. Such an inclusive emphasis does not ignore the fact that recognising difference within the college community has significant resource implications. This will involve difficult management decisions and prioritising from limited funding. Treating marginalised groups as an afterthought or as a low priority on the marketable scale of cost-effectiveness needs to be challenged. The creation of whole-college policies is of utmost importance in this context. It needs to be one of the vehicles through which senior management, especially principals, give a leading role. Not only must their responsibility be to see that such policies are created but also they have to ensure that the necessary monitoring and evaluation procedures are established. These must be given sufficient power to secure the effective working of such policies. Ad hoc, ill-conceived endeavours or reliance on a charismatic individual, features of much past practice, is unacceptable if quality assurance is to be guaranteed.

In a report of two conferences held in England in 1991, relating to employment opportunities for people with severe learning difficulties, the following issue was seen as an agenda item for future discussion and action:

> We need a vision of the desirable future for people with learning difficulties which will often be radically different from how their lives appear now.
>
> (Wertheimer, 1991, p. 51)

We endorse this and maintain that sources of inspiration and ideas may be derived from policies and practices outside our own country. Different perspectives, emerging from contrasting cultural contexts, can present a refreshing, yet disturbing, challenge to 'reality'. Comparative accounts need to be shared and this clearly is an urgent future agenda for change. Valuable evidence of cross-cultural developments and insights have recently been published (e.g. Fulcher, 1989; Daunt, 1991; OECD, 1991; McGinty and Fish, 1992). They can often prove uncomfortable reading, for what is regarded as 'impractical' in Britain may be quite workable elsewhere. We need to be open to adopting 'radically different' approaches if they involve the empowerment of marginalised groups.

If 'radically different' approaches are to be promulgated, this requires a challenge to the status quo. We began our book with an examination of some critical comments on the Government White Paper *Education and Training for the 21st Century* (DES, 1991a). People with special educational needs appeared to be marginalised yet again within this new legislation. One of the most offensive omissions was that of recognising the implications of the *Care in the Community* initiative. On the one hand, the Government promoted community care; on the other it failed to provide the network of support services essential for effective implementation. As the Danish 'Kurator' system so clearly illustrates, continuity and close liaison between services is an integral component of quality provision. At a Conference in November 1991, Deborah Cooper, the Director of Skill: The National Bureau for Students with Disabilities, said:

> According to the Undersecretary in the Department of Health, they should be liaising widely and talking to Education Services because Care in the Community is all about using educational institutions. But, according to a letter I received from the Department of Health, they don't have to do so because it was not written into the Bill. They may, if the college thinks they are providing day care facilities. I don't think colleges feel they are providing day care facilities. They probably think they are providing educational services, which may well be a very important part of someone's 'Community Care Plan'. I think that the link between Social Services and Education is absolutely crucial and the evidence we have is that it is very patchy.
>
> (Cooper, 1991)

Cooper's observations reflect that struggle for choice which has been the primary concern of our book. Issues that are 'crucial' to the well-being of disabled people and people with learning difficulties are not satisfactorily addressed, for provision continues to be 'patchy'. We have tried to demonstrate some of the frustrations and injustices which arise when 'crucial' needs are met by 'patchy' services. Our perspective is that a struggle for choice is unacceptable. It is a continual burden upon an already disadvantaged group in society.

We want to end our book with the perceptions and feelings

of disabled people and people with learning difficulties. It is they who experience the struggle for choice. For many of them, the transition from school to college, work or training and the move from dependent to independent status in the community is stressful and frustrating. They face barriers which are beyond their control.

Job choices are often restricted. For deaf school leavers, their opportunities are reliant on good careers guidance and supportive employers. Sometimes they find a job which suits them but often they have to settle for undemanding, boring tasks which frustrate them. The job of a stone-mason, for example, which is focused upon manual dexterity rather than verbal skills, was satisfying for one deaf young man:

> It's a very interesting job really. You get lots of design come-back. You have to think the job out yourself. OK so you may get help from the foreman or someone else who knows a bit more than you would, but on the whole it is interesting. It is quite fascinating.

But another noted:

> They pick on me and make me sweep up – I only get a poor wage. I looked for another job for two months but now I'm not bothered. I will stay at the same firm although there is no training. I'd like to work abroad like in 'Auf Wieder-sehen Pet' but I don't think that will happen because I'm deaf.
>
> (quoted in Bishop *et al.*, 1991, p. 138)

The authors reflected 'at least in the early years of their working lives, that the majority of young people were in a limited range of manual jobs in which they felt frustrated and from which they did not think they could or should attempt to move' (p. 139).

As we have demonstrated in the examples we have chosen throughout the book, 'special educational need' is a broad and nebulous term. It includes those young people whose 'learning difficulties' may stem from a strong resistance to any form of schooling. Their choices may be highly pragmatic:

> I never went to school anyway so I didn't know the proper

leaving date. I got behind with GCSE coursework and I'd never catch up so there weren't any point. When I left school there was nowt for me. It were in between computers and skilled labour so I thought I might as well have a baby and settle down to that.

(quoted in Ainley, 1991, p. 47)

Ainley's report of the experiences of young people leaving home illustrates the many contributory factors which effectively limit their choices and determine their options. Class, gender and race issues are clearly significant factors in relation to the struggle for choices in housing, employment and further education or training.

Prejudice, on the grounds of class, race or gender, is well established but recent findings of the experiences shared by disabled people suggest that responses to their disability are not always sympathetic. This disabled trainer in Disability Equality found that

The hostility was not directed towards me as an individual but towards disabled people. I never dreamed that there was such a subconscious, *and* conscious, degree of hatred – the hatred expressed by the people I was training was far more powerful than their patronising attitudes. I was really surprised and shocked. I had come from such a traditional background of experiencing patronisation. And to come from that to realise that I was also a person who was hated.

(Moore, quoted in Morris, 1991, pp. 22–3)

It seems that overt hostility rests just underneath a surface sympathy. To a certain extent, the fact that Disability Equality training by disabled people has revealed such prejudice can be viewed as positively healthy. Let us admit our dislike of difference and not pretend to feel any more than pity or remorse. Mottley's (1991) autobiographical account of her experiences, which included giving birth to and bringing up a child with disabilities resulting from Thalidomide, is unique in its honesty. She actively disliked what her daughter became, perceiving the disability as having created her selfishness, tyranny and greed. Both this stance and that of a public hatred of disability is part of the 'reality' in disabled people's lives. Perhaps it is now healthier that such distaste is openly exposed. Until prejudices are faced and until it is acknowledged that not all disabled people fit a passive, gentle stereotype, disabled people will be seen as a distinct species, with separate feelings and needs.

In his autobiographical account of a harsh Irish schooling, Doyle (1988) describes how frustrating it was to be expected to deny himself expectations of a full community life just because of his disability:

> In 1974, I got married. Many objected to the idea and voiced their total disagreement to a disabled man marrying an able-bodied woman. People took my wife aside and warned her that she would end up 'looking after' me. What infuriated me most about these interfering busybodies was their blatant disregard for the good sense of either my wife or myself.
>
> (Doyle, 1988, p. 203)

It would be comfortable to assume that such an intrusive level of interference was typical of that period and would no longer be a regular occurrence. Yet, Morris (1989) recounts her experience, with a rather different emphasis, of being asked by the doctor advising her to ensure that she had the support of a male partner as she could not possibly cope alone. In both instances, the 'good sense' of those making such choices seems to be completely ignored in a short-sighted focus on disability and its negative impact.

It would be a distorted reflection of current developments if we were to conclude the book on a purely negative note. There is still a real struggle for rights and dignity. However, considerable advances have been made at all levels. The issue of 'curriculum entitlement' is now on the FE agenda and there are many who will struggle to keep it there despite legislative pressures. Many are also learning how to use the system, typified now by the power and wealth of the TECs, to their own advantage. Disabled people, like Morris (1991), are fostering positive images of themselves, celebrating difference and not hiding from it. In their powerful collection of prose and poetry by people with learning difficulties, Atkinson and Williams (1990) demonstrate the strengths and assertions of a previously silent minority. This includes women with learning difficulties forming a Women's Group 'to talk about things that are important to women' (p. 172) and a choir who perform for the public because 'We are not stupid, we're not daft and we can sing' (p. 176). Reading accounts of people with learning difficulties who are living in flats in the community, who are married, have jobs and help others can offer an insight into just how far we have advanced from the punitive, custodial model of the recent past.

It has been our intention in this book to convey something of the struggle involved in assuming an adult role in society when your status is marginalised through disability. We are aware of the progression to date and the considerable battles which have been won. Our concern is to avoid complacency. There are many issues still to be resolved if disabled people and those marginalised through experience of educational failure are to be offered meaningful choices in transition to adulthood. Choices have to be contextualised. They are rarely without compromises for any of us. For those who have been the focus of this book, tangible choices tend to emerge only from a degree of conflict.

APPENDIX

Further education colleges were designed primarily to serve 16–19 years olds, with a focus on training programmes and vocational preparation rather than exclusively academic courses. One of the distinctive features of these colleges is that through the range of routes they offer they can cater for a diversity of needs. They relate to higher education, adult education and secondary education by linking with each sector in various ways.

FURTHER EDUCATION AND HIGHER EDUCATION

Students in further education can attend what are termed 'Access' courses which prepare them for entry into higher education. These courses are particularly relevant to mature learners and those without traditional academic qualifications. In this sense, further education provides a ladder which leads to degree-level qualifications.

FURTHER AND ADULT EDUCATION

The relationship between further education and adult education varies from area to area in Britain. In some instances these two aspects of education provision have developed separately, whilst in other areas they have been incorporated. Adult education has traditionally maintained a different character from further education, being more concerned with recreational interests and non-vocational courses. This form of provision has often been receptive to the inclusion of adults with learning difficulties.

The distinction between adult education and further education is now becoming more ambiguous. The effect of recent legislation, specifically the government white paper *Education and Training for the 21st Century* (DES, 1971), has altered the nature and relationship of these two forms of provision. Further education colleges will be expected to take on complex additional areas of responsibility, which include adult education.

FURTHER EDUCATION AND SECONDARY EDUCATION

Further education colleges have close liaison with their local secondary schools. This involves the provision of courses for pupils in their last two years of compulsory schooling, i.e. 14–16 years. Students can attend a range of prevocational courses which are designed to associate technical training and work preparation with secondary education.

Further education colleges also serve special schools by offering link courses for their school leavers. The age range is from 15 to 19 years depending upon the nature of the specific school. Link courses are designed to introduce these students to college and to prepare them for attendance on full-time courses.

FURTHER EDUCATION AND TRAINING PROGRAMMES

Within their recently expanding range of responsibilities, further education colleges have offered training elements for government training programmes. These are programmes designed specifically for individuals who have been deemed in need of preparation for employment. They attend college, either full-time or for a period of time every week during their training, to receive college-based vocational teaching. In some instances, the college staff go off site to deliver training in the training work-base.

THE ROLE OF FURTHER EDUCATION

Overall, the role of further education in the British educational system is becoming increasingly complex. It is linked to higher education as a feeder-process, to adult education as a collaborator, to training programmes as an integral part of the provision and to secondary schools as an introduction to secondary education. Thus it can be seen to play a central role in a complex educational network.

POSTSCRIPT

Offering suggested readings is a precarious business especially as literature often becomes very dated. Nevertheless, there are some texts on FE post–16 issues generally which ought to be read by all those interested in this sphere of educational provision. They include:

Ainley, P. (1988) *From School to YTS: Education and Training in England and Wales, 1944–1987*. Milton Keynes: Open University Press.

Chitty, C. (ed.) (1991) *Post–16 Education: Studies in Access and Achievement*. London: Kogan Page.

Coles, B. (ed.) (1988) *Young Careers: The Search for Jobs and the New Vocationalism*. Milton Keynes: Open University Press.

Gleeson, D. (1989) *The Paradox of Training: Making Progress out of Crisis*. Milton Keynes: Open University Press.

McGinty, J. and Fish, J. (1992) *Learning Support for Young People in Transition: Leaving School for Further Education and Work*. Milton Keynes: Open University Press.

Wallace, C. (1987) *For Richer For Poorer: Growing Up In and Out of Work*. London: Tavistock.

Willis, P., Betenn, P., Ellis, T. and Whitt, D. (1988) *Youth Review: Social Conditions of Young People in Wolverhampton*. Aldershot: Gower.

REFERENCES

INTRODUCTION

Ainley, P. (1990) *Vocation, Education and Training*. London: Cassell.

Bradley, J. (ed.) (1985) *From Coping to Confidence*. London: Further Education Unit (FEU/National Foundation for Educational Research (NFER).

Brenchley, J. (1991) 'Muddling to the Millennium', *Times Educational Supplement*, 5 July, p. 16.

Cooper, D. (1989) *An Opportunity for Change*. London: Skill.

Dee, L. (1988) 'Young People with Severe Learning Difficulties in Colleges of Further Education: Some Current Issues', *Journal of Further and Higher Education*, vol. 12, no. 2, pp. 12–21.

DES (1991a) *Education and Training for the 21st Century, Cm 1536*. London: HMSO.

Faraday, S. and Harris, R. (1989) *Learning Support*. Sheffield: Training Agency/ Skill/ FEU.

Gleeson, D. (ed.) (1990) *Training and its Alternatives*. Milton Keynes: Open University Press.

Hollands, R. (1990) *The Long Transition: Class, Culture and Youth Training*. Basingstoke: Macmillan.

Maclure, S. (1991) *Missing Links: The Challenge to Further Education*. London: Policy Studies Institute.

Oliver, M. (1990) *The Politics of Disablement*. London: Macmillan.

Stowell, R. (1987) *Catching Up?* London: National Bureau for Handicapped Students.

Sutcliffe, J. (1990) *Adults with Learning Difficulties: Education for Choice and Empowerment*. Leicester: National Institute of Adult Continuing Education (NIACE)/Open University Press.

TES (1991) 'Afterthoughts which Ignore New Beginnings', *Times Educational Supplement*, 5 July, p. 17.

1 SETTING THE SCENE

Abberley, P. (1987) 'The Concept of Oppression and the Development of a Social Theory of Disability', *Disability, Handicap and Society*, vol. 2, no. 1, pp. 5–20.

Ainley, P. (1988) *From School to YTS: Education and Training in England and Wales, 1944–1987.* Milton Keynes: Open University Press.

Ainley, P. (1990) *Vocational Education and Training.* London: Cassell.

Ainley, P. and Corney, M. (1990) *Training for the Future: The Rise and Fall of the Manpower Services Commission.* London: Cassell.

Beloff, H. (ed.) (1986) *Getting into Life.* London: Methuen.

Bradley, J. (ed.) (1985) *From Coping to Confidence.* London: FEU/ DES/ NFER.

Bradley, J. and Hegarty, S. (1981) *Students with Special Needs in FE.* London: Further Education Unit.

Brown, P. (1988) 'The New Vocationalism: A Policy for Inequality?', in Coles, B. (ed.) *Young Careers: The Search for Jobs and the New Vocationalism.* Milton Keynes: Open University Press.

Carr, W. (1986) 'Theories of Theory and Practice', *Journal of Philosophy of Education*, vol. 20, no. 2, pp. 177–86.

Cockburn, C. (1987) *Two-Track Training: Sex Inequalities and the YTS.* Basingstoke: Macmillan Education.

Coles, B. (1988) 'Youth Unemployment and the Growth of "New Vocationalism"', in Coles, B. (ed.) *Young Careers: The Search for Jobs and the New Vocationalism.* Milton Keynes: Open University Press.

Corbett, J. (1987) 'Integration in Further Education: A Case Study', Unpublished Ph.D, Open University.

Corbett, J. (1990a) *Providing for Special Needs: Policy and Practice.* Diploma in Post-Compulsory Education, E877, Milton Keynes: Open University Press.

Corbett, J. (1990b) 'It's Almost Like Work: A Study of a YTS Workshop', in Corbett, J. (ed.) *Uneasy Transitions: Disaffection in Post-compulsory Education and Training.* Lewes: Falmer Press.

Cross, M. and Smith, D. (1987) *Black Youth Futures: Ethnic Minorities and the Youth Training Scheme.* London: National Youth Bureau.

Cunningham, K. (1990) 'Talent Leaking Away', *Times Educational Supplement*, 17 August, p. 10.

Dean, C. (1990) 'Labour says Cuts Send Youth into Twilight Zone', *Times Educational Supplement*, 17 August, p. 6.

Dee, L. (1988) *New Directions.* London: Further Education Unit (FEU)/National Foundation for Educational Research (NFER).

DES (1987) *A 'Special' Professionalism.* London: HMSO.

DES (1989) *Students with Special Needs in Further Education*, London: HMSO.

DES (1990) *Work-based Learning in Further Education.* London: HMSO.

DES (1991a) *Education and Training for the 21st Century, Cm 1536.* London: HMSO.

Dessent, T. (1987) *Making the Ordinary School Special.* Lewes: Falmer Press.

Dickinson, H., and Erben, M. (1989) 'Young Adults: The Nature of Work and Vocational Preparation', *Journal of Further and Higher Education*, vol. 13, no. 1, pp. 46–53.

Dyson, A. (1990) 'Special Educational Needs and the Concept of Change', *Oxford Review of Education*, vol. 16, no. 1, pp. 55–66.

Evetts, J. (1973) *The Sociology of Educational Ideas*. London: Routledge and Kegan Paul.

Faraday, S. and Harris, R. (1989) *Learning Support*. Sheffield: Training Agency/ Skill/ FEU.

Fenton, S. and Burton, P. (1987) 'YTS and Equal Opportunity Policy', in Cross, M. and Smith, D. (eds) *Black Youth Futures: Ethnic Minorities and the Youth Training Scheme*. London: National Youth Bureau.

FEU (1989a) *Towards a Framework for Curriculum Entitlement*: London: Further Education Unit.

FEU (1989b) *Supporting Quality in YTS*. London: Further Education Unit.

Finegold, D. and Soskice, D. (1990) 'The Failure of Training in Britain: Analysis and Prescription', in Gleeson, D. (ed.) *Training and its Alternatives*. Milton Keynes: Open University Press.

Fulcher, G. (1989) *Disabling Policies? A Comparative Approach to Education Policy and Disability*. Lewes: Falmer Press.

Ghua, E. (1988) 'Exploring Equality in Black and White', *Youth Training News*, no. 49, p. 8, Sheffield: Training Agency.

Gleeson, D. (ed.) (1990a) *Training and its Alternatives*. Milton Keynes: Open University Press.

Gleeson, D. (1990b) 'Skills Training and its Alternatives', in Gleeson, D. (ed.) *Training and its Alternatives*. Milton Keynes: Open University Press.

Green, A. (1990) 'The Price of Educational Fragmentation After 16', in *Comprehensive Education and Training from 16 Plus*. London: Campaign for the Advancement of State Education (CASE).

Hollands, R. (1990) *The Long Transition: Class, Culture and Youth Training*. Basingstoke: Macmillan.

Hutchinson, D. and Tennyson, C. (1986) *Transition to Adulthood*. London: Further Education Unit.

Jackson, M. (1990) 'Eager to Shake Hands with a One-time Pariah', *Times Educational Supplement*, 6 July, p. 10.

Kedney, B. (1988) 'The Changing Environment of the Colleges', in Parkes, D. (ed.) *Managing a Changing FE*. London: Longman for the Further Education Unit.

Leach, B. (1989) 'Disabled People and the Implication of Local Authorities Equal Opportunities Policies', *Public Administration*, Spring, pp. 65–78.

McKie, L. (1990) 'The Youth Training Scheme: the Panacea of the 1980s, the Liability of the 1990s?', *Youth and Policy*, no. 30, pp. 8–20.

Mills, C.W. (1970) *The Sociological Imagination*. Harmondsworth: Penguin.

Newton, J. and Robinson, J. (1982) *Special School Leavers: The Value of Further Education in their Transition to the Adult World*. London: Greater London Association for the Disabled (GLAD).

NUT (1990a) *A Strategy for the Curriculum*. London: National Union of Teachers.

NUT (1990b) *Special Education and Post 16 Students.* London: National Union of Teachers.

Oliver, M. (1990) *The Politics of Disablement.* Basingstoke: Macmillan Education.

Plunkett, D. (1987) 'Values and Propaganda in 14–19 Education', in *The Policies of Progress? Contemporary Issues in Educational Change.* University of Southampton: Department of Education and Adult Education.

Rosie, A. (1988) 'An Ethnographic Study of a YTS Course', in Pollard, A., Purvis, J. and Walford, G. (eds) *Education, Training and the New Vocationalism.* Milton Keynes: Open University Press.

Stowell, R. (1987) *Catching Up?* London: National Bureau for Handicapped Students (now Skill: The National Bureau for Students with Disabilities).

2 ADULTHOOD

Bagley, B. (1988) 'North Manchester College: a Rolling Stone', in Parkes, D. (ed.) *Managing a Changing FE.* London: Further Education Unit.

Barnard, N. and Linehan, (1989) *Community Access Project.* London: Community Services volunteers.

Barnes, C. (1990) *'Cabbage Syndrome': The Social Construction of Dependence.* Lewes: Falmer Press.

Barton, L. (1986) 'The Politics of Special Educational Needs', *Disability, Handicap and Society,* vol. 1, no. 3, pp. 273–90.

Booth, T. (1988) 'Challenging Conceptions of Integration', in Barton, L. (ed.) *The Politics of Special Educational Needs.* Lewes: Falmer Press.

Brown, H. and Smith, H. (1989) 'Whose "Ordinary Life" is it Anyway?', *Disability, Handicap and Society,* vol. 4, no. 2, pp. 105–20.

Campbell, D. (1990) 'The Forces of Prejudice', *Guardian Society,* 31 October, p. 23.

Carnie, C. (1990) 'Changes in Social Education Centres: Aspects of Disaffection', in Corbett, J. (ed.) *Uneasy Transitions: Disaffection in Post-compulsory Education and Training.* Lewes: Falmer Press.

Cattermole, M., Jahorde, A. and Markova, I. (1990) 'Quality of Life for People with Learning Difficulties Moving to Community Homes', *Disability, Handicap and Society,* vol. 5, no. 2, pp. 137–52

Chapman, L. (1988) 'Disabling Services', *Educare,* no. 31, pp. 15–20.

Clare, M. (1990) *Developing Self-Advocacy Skills with People with Disabilities and Learning Difficulties.* London: Further Education Unit.

Corbett, J. (1990) 'It's Almost Like Work: A Study of a YTS Workshop', in Corbett, J. (ed.) *Uneasy Transitions: Disaffection in Post-compulsory Education and Training.* Lewes: Falmer Press.

Fenton, S. and Burton, P. (1987) 'YTS and Equal Opportunity Policy' in Cross, M. and Smith, D. (eds) *Black Youth Futures: Ethnic Minorities and the Youth Training Scheme.* London: National Youth Bureau.

Fenton, M. and Hughes, P. (1989) *Passivity to Empowerment: A Living Skills Curriculum for People with Disabilities.* London: Royal Association for Disability and Rehabilitation (RADAR).

Firth, H. and Rapley, M. (1990) *From Acquaintance to Friendship: Issues for People with Learning Difficulties.* Kidderminster: British Institute of Mental Handicap (BIMH).

Fish, J. (1990) 'Collaboration and Co-operation: the Road to Adulthood', *Educare*, no. 37, pp. 3–6.

Gray, J., Jesson, D., Pattie, C. and Sime, N. (1989) *England and Wales Youth Cohort Study: Education and Training Opportunities in the Inner-City.* Sheffield: Training Agency.

Griffiths, M. (1989) *Enabled to Work.* London: Further Education Unit.

Hamilton, M. (1989) *Learning for Life.* Manchester: Rathbone Society.

John, M. (1986) *Disabled Young People Living Independently.* London: British Council of Organisations of Disabled People.

Katoda, H. and Miron, G. (1990) 'Educational Integration for Persons with Handicaps: a Conceptual Discussion', *European Journal of Special Needs Education*, vol. 5, no. 2, pp. 126–34.

Mason, M. (1986) *Beyond the Label of Physical Disability: In Our Own Right*, London: Community Services volunteers.

Phillips, A. (1990) 'Giro Land', *Guardian*, 27 October, pp. 4–7.

Tomlinson, S. (1982) *A Sociology of Special Education.* London: Routledge and Kegan Paul.

Trower, P., Bryant, B. and Argyle, M. (1978) *Social Skills and Mental Health.* London: Methuen.

Unwin, L. (1990) 'Learning to Live Underwater', in Flude, M. and Hammer, M. (eds) *The Education Reform Act 1988: Its Origins and Implications.* Lewes: Falmer Press.

Whelan, E., Speake, B. and Strickland, T. (1984) 'The Copewell Curriculum: Development, Content and Use', in Dean, A. and Hegarty, S. (eds) *Learning for Independence.* London: Further Education Unit.

Wilkinson, A. (1990) 'Complicated Lives: Students with Special Needs in the Inner-City', in Corbett, J. (ed.) *Uneasy Transitions: Disaffection in Post-compulsory Education and Training.* Lewes: Falmer Press.

Wilkinson, J. and Canter, S. (1982) *Social Skills Training Manual: Assessment Program Design and Management of Training.* London: Wiley.

Wolfensberger, W. (1975) *The Origin and Nature of our Institutional Models*, Syracuse: Human Policy Press.

Wolfensberger, W. (1989) 'Human Service Policies: The Rhetoric Versus the Reality', in Barton, L. (ed.) *Disability and Dependency.* Lewes: Falmer Press.

Woods, S. and Shears, B. (1986) *Teaching Children with Severe Learning Difficulties: A Radical Reappraisal.* Beckenham: Croom Helm.

3 CURRICULUM ISSUES

Ainscow, M. (1991) 'Becoming a Reflective Teacher', in Booth, T., Swann, W., Masterton, M. and Potts, P. (eds) *Curricula for Diversity in Education.* London: Routledge.

Ainscow, M. and Tweddle, D. (1979) *Preventing Classroom Failure: An Objective Approach.* London: Fulton.

REFERENCES

Ainscow, M. and Tweddle, D. (1984) *Early Learning Skills Analysis.* London: Fulton.

Ainscow, M. and Tweddle, D. (1988) *Encouraging Classroom Success.* London: Fulton.

Apple, M. (1990) *Ideology and Curriculum.* London: Routledge (2nd edition).

Atkinson, D. and Brechin, A. (1989) *Patterns for Living: Working Together.* Milton Keynes: Open University Press.

Blunden, R. and Allen D. (1987) *Facing the Challenge.* London: King's Fund Centre.

Bradley, J. (ed.) (1985) *From Coping to Confidence.* London: FEU/DES/NFER.

Connelly, N. (1990) *Between Apathy and Outrage.* London: Policy Studies Institute.

Corbett, J. (1991) 'Moving On: Training for Community Living', *Educare.*

Crook, M. (1988) 'Care and Education: Planning for People Moving Out of Long-Stay Institutions', in *Innovations in Education for Adults with Special Needs.* London: Skill.

Daniels, H. (1990) 'The Modified Curriculum: Help with the Same or Something Completely Different?', in Evans, P. and Varma, V. (eds) *Special Education: Past, Present and Future.* Lewes: Falmer Press.

Dee, L. (1988) 'Young People with Severe Learning Difficulties in Colleges of Further Education: Some Current Issues', *Journal of Further and Higher Education*, vol. 12, no. 2, pp. 12–21.

Dowson, S. (1990) *Keeping it Safe.* London: Values into Action.

FEU (1982) *Skills for Living.* London: Further Education Unit.

Flude, M. and Hammer M. (eds) (1990) *The Education Reform Act 1988: Its Origins and Implications.* Lewes: Falmer Press.

Hargreaves, A. (1989) *Curriculum and Assessment Reform.* Milton Keynes: Open University Press.

Kedney, B. and Parkes, D. (1988) *Planning the FE Curriculum: Implications of the 1988 Education Reform Act.* London: Further Education Unit.

Lumb, K. (1990) 'The Drama of Disability in Charity Fundraising', *Coalition*, December, pp. 4–13.

NCC (1990) *Education for Citizenship.* York: National Curriculum Council.

Richardson, A. and Ritchie, J. (1989) *Developing Friendships.* London: Policy Studies Institute.

Roe, N. (1990) 'A real chance to love thy neighbour', *The Independent*, 22 November, p. 20.

Seed, P. and Montgomery, B. (1989) *Towards Independent Living.* London: Jessica Kingsley.

Sutcliffe, J. (1990) *Adults with Learning Difficulties: Education for Choice and Empowerment.* Leicester: National Institute of Adult Continuing Education (NIACE)/Open University Press.

Wallace, J. (1990) *Providing for Adults.* London: Further Education Unit.

Wertheimer, A. (1988) *According to the Papers: Press Reporting on People with Learning Difficulties*, London: Campaign for the Mentally Handicapped (CMH).

West, H. (1986) 'Love me as I am', in Corbett, J. (ed.) (1989) *Choices After 16*. Milton Keynes: Open University Press.

Whelan, E. and Speake, B. (1979) *Learning to Cope*. London: Souvenir Press.

Whitty, G. (1989) 'The New Right and the National Curriculum: State Control or Market Forces', *Journal of Education Policy*, vol. 4, no. 4, pp. 329–41.

4 VOCATIONALISM: EXPERIENCES AND OPPORTUNITIES

Ainley, P. (1988) *From School to YTS: Education and Training in England and Wales 1944–1987*. Milton Keynes: Open University Press.

Ainley, P. (1990) *Vocational Education and Training*. London: Cassell.

Barnes, C. (1990) *'Cabbage Syndrome': The Social Construction of Dependence*. Lewes: Falmer Press.

Barton, L. (ed.) (1989) *Disability and Dependency*. Lewes: Falmer Press.

Begum, N. (1990) *Burden of Gratitude: Women with Disabilities Receiving Personal Care*. Coventry: University of Warwick.

Borsay, A. (1986) 'Personal Trouble or Public Issue? Towards a Model of Policy for People with Physical and Mental Disabilities', *Disability, Handicap and Society*, vol. 1, no. 2, pp. 179–96.

Cooper, D. (1988) *Building on Ability*. London: Further Education Unit.

Corbett, J. (1990) 'It's Almost Like Work: A Study of a YTS Workshop', in Corbett, J. (ed.) *Uneasy Transitions: Disaffection in Post-Compulsory Education and Training*. Lewes: Falmer Press.

Dalley, G. (1989) 'Community Care: the Ideal and the Reality', in Brechin, A. and Walmsley, J. (eds.) *Making Connections*. London: Hodder and Stoughton.

Davis, A. (1989) *From Where I Sit*. London: Triangle.

Evans, G. and Murcott, A. (1990) 'Community Care: Relationships and Control', *Disability, Handicap and Society*, vol. 5, no. 2, pp. 123–36.

Firth, H. and Rapley, M. (1990) *From Acquaintance to Friendship: Issues for People with Learning Difficulties*. Kidderminster: British Institute of Mental Handicap (BIMH).

Fraser, R. (ed.) (1969) *Work: volume 2. Twenty Personal Accounts*. Harmondsworth: Penguin.

Gleeson, D. (1989) *The Paradox of Training: Making Progress Out of Crisis*. Milton Keynes: Open University Press.

Griffiths, M. (1989) *Enabled to Work: Support into Employment for Young People with Disabilities*. London: Further Education Unit.

Hollands, R. (1990) *The Long Transition: Class, Culture and Youth Training*. Basingstoke: Macmillan.

Holt, M. (ed.) (1987) *Skills and Vocationalism: The Easy Answers*. Milton Keynes: Open University Press.

Keith, L. (1992) 'Who Cares Wins? Women, Caring and Disability', in *Disability, Handicap and Society* (forthcoming Special Issue).

Newman, S. (ed.) (1990) *Workmates: A Study of Employment Opportunities for Disabled People*. Bishop's Stortford: Mainstream.

Oliver, M. (1989) 'Disability and Dependency: A Creation of Industrial Societies', in Barton, L. (ed.) *Disability and Dependency*. Lewes: Falmer Press.

Parsons, K. (1990) 'Trainers and Tutors in the YTS Environment', in Wallace, C. and Cross, M. (eds.) *Youth in Transition: The Sociology of Youth and Youth Policy*. Lewes: Falmer Press.

Raffe, D. (1990) 'The Transition from YTS to Work: Content, Context and the External Labour Market', in Wallace, C. and Cross, M. (eds.) *Youth in Transition: The Sociology of Youth and Youth Policy*. Lewes: Falmer Press.

Richardson, A. and Ritchie, J. (1989) *Developing Friendships*. London: Policy Studies Institute.

Shilling, C. (1989) *Schooling for Work in Capitalist Britain*. Lewes: Falmer Press.

Spours, K. and Young, M. (1988) 'Beyond Vocationalism: A New Perspective on the Relationship Between Work and Education', *British Journal of Education and Work*, vol. 2, no. 2, pp. 5–14.

Sutcliffe, J. (1990) *Adults with Learning Difficulties: Education for Choice and Empowerment*. Leicester: National Institute of Adult Continuing Education (NIACE)/Open University Press.

Vincent, A, (ed.) (1989) *New Technology, Disability and Special Educational Needs: Some Case Studies*. Coventry: Empathy Ltd.

Williams, M. (1991) 'Cyrus's Pathway to Success', *MENCAP News*, April, pp. 4–5.

5 DIFFERENCES IN THE COMMUNITY

Barber, L. (1990) 'Lucky Enough to Even the Score' (interview with Jeffrey Tate), *Independent Magazine*, 8 July, pp. 8–10.

Barnes, C. (1990) '*Cabbage Syndrome*': *The Social Construction of Dependence*. Lewes: Falmer Press.

Booth, T. (1987) 'Labels and their Consequences', in Lane, D. and Stratford, B. (eds) *Current Approaches to Down's Syndrome*. London: Cassell.

Bradley, J. (ed.) (1985) *From Coping to Confidence*. London: DES/FEU/NFER.

Brown, R. (1988) 'Transition: A Challenge for School, Agency and Community', *Australia and New Zealand Journal of Developmental Disabilities*, vol. 14, nos 3 and 4, pp. 227–34.

Cheaney, M. (1990) 'Body Blow', *Guardian*, 27 March, p. 45.

Corbett, J. (1991) 'Reflections on Training Programmes by Trainees', unpublished report for the Further Education Unit.

Duffy, M. (1990) 'Asking For It', in Rieser, R. and Mason, M. (eds.)

Disability Equality in the Classroom: A Human Rights Issue. London: Inner London Education Authority (ILEA).

Edgerton, R. (1967) *The Cloak of Competence*. Berkeley: University of California Press.

Farrell, E. (1990) 'Finding a Voice: Women with Learning Difficulties in Camden'. B.Sc. by Independent Study, Polytechnic of East London.

Fenton, M. and Hughes, P. (1989) *Passivity to Empowerment*. London: Royal Association for Disability and Rehabilitation (RADAR).

FEU (1987) *FE in Black and White*. London: Longman for the Further Education Unit.

FEU (1990) *Perceptions of Special Needs in Further Education*. London: Further Education Unit.

Firth, H. and Rapley, M. (1990) *From Acquaintance to Friendship: Issues for People with Learning Difficulties*. Kidderminster: British Institute of Mental Handicap (BIMH).

Goffman, E. (1968) *Stigma*. Harmondsworth: Penguin.

Lynch, J. (1987) *Prejudice Reduction and the Schools*. London: Cassell.

Mann, E. (1939) *School for Barbarians: Education under the Nazis*. London: Lindsay Drummond.

O'Brien, J. and Mount, B. (1990) 'Telling New Stories: the Search for Capacity among People with Severe Handicap', in Meyer, L., Peck, C. and Brown, L. (eds) *Critical Issues in the Lives of People with Severe Disabilities*. Baltimore, Maryland: Paul Brooks.

Richardson, A. and Ritchie, J. (1989) *Developing Friendships*. London: Policy Studies Institute.

Taylor, P. (1990) 'Life Fulfilment of Filling in Time?', in Woolrych, R. (ed.) *Developing Day Services*. Ross-on-Wye: Association of Professions for Mentally Handicapped People.

Turnham, M. (1992) 'Supporting Special Needs in Further Education', in Booth, T., Swann, M., Masterton, M. and Potts, P. (eds.) *Policies for Diversity in Education*. London: Routledge.

Vasey, S. (1990) 'Disability Culture: It's a Way of Life', in Rieser, R. and Mason, M. (eds.) *Disability Equality in the Classroom: A Human Rights Issue*. London: Inner London Education Authority (ILEA).

6 EQUAL OPPORTUNITIES

Cooper, D. (1988) *An Opportunity for Change*. London: Skill.

Corbett, J. (1987) 'Integration in Further Education: a Case Study'. Unpublished Ph.D, Open University.

DES (1987) *A 'Special' Professionalism*. London: HMSO.

DES (1991a) *Education and Training for the 21st Century*, Cm 1536. London: HMSO.

DES (1991b) *Transition from School to Further Education for Students with Learning Difficulties*. London: DES.

Edwards, R. (1991) 'The Politics of Meeting Learner Needs: Power, Subject and Subjection', *Studies in the Education of Adults*, vol. 23, no. 1, pp. 85–97.

FEU (1990) *Perspectives of Specialness in Further Education*. London: FEU Bulletin.

Harries, W. (1990) 'Students with severe learning difficulties and social integration', in Open University Diploma in Post Compulsory Education (Part B) *Offprint Book 6*. Milton Keynes: Open University Press.

Hutchinson, D. and Tennyson, C. (1986) *Transition to Adulthood*. London: Further Education Unit.

INSIGHT (1991) 'NVQs and Flexible Learning', *INSIGHT*, no. 22, pp. 28–31.

Molloy, M. (1991) 'Developing Individual Service Plans for People with Severe Disabilities', in OECD, *Disabled Youth: From School to Work*. Paris: OECD.

Morris, J. (1987) 'Progress with Humanity? : the Experience of a Disabled Lecturer', in Booth, T. and Swann, W. (eds) *Including Pupils with Disabilities*. Milton Keynes: Open University Press.

Morris, J. (ed.) (1990) *Able Lives*. London: The Women's Press.

Nelson, A. (1991) 'Tertiary Organisation Structures', *Journal of Further and Higher Education*, vol. 15, no. 1, pp. 80–8.

OECD (1991) *Disabled Youth: From School to Work*. Paris: OECD.

O'Grady, C. (1990) 'Kingsway College Post–16 Provision', in *Integration Working*. London: Centre for Studies in Integration in Education (CSIE).

Rieser, R. (1990) 'Internalised Oppression: How It Seems to Me', in Rieser, R. and Mason, M. (eds) *Disability Equality in the Classroom: A Human Rights Issue*. London: Inner London Education Authority (ILEA).

Van Dyke, R. (1990) 'Equal Opportunities Practices in the Open University', in *Equal Opportunities in Practice: A Staff Development Day*. London Region: Open University.

Wardman, P. (1990) 'An investigation into the implementation of Southwark College's policy on equal opportunities for students with special educational needs', in Open University Diploma in Post Compulsory Education (Part B) *Offprint Book 6*. Milton Keynes: Open University Press.

Whittaker, J. (1991) 'Inclusive education for a more creative and effective further education service', *Educare*, no. 39, pp. 24–6.

7 CO-ORDINATORS IN A PROCESS OF CHANGE

Blake, M. and Blake, D. (1988) 'Curriculum Change and the Responses of Lecturers in Further Education to Students with Special Educational Needs', *Journal of Further and Higher Education*, vol. 12, no. 3, pp. 80–7.

Bradley, J. (ed.) (1985) *From Coping to Confidence*. London: DES/FEU/NFER.

Cassara, B. (ed.) (1990) *Adult Education in a Multicultural Society*. London: Routledge.

Fennell, E. (1991) 'TEC tonics', DES *Pickup in Progress*, no. 25, pp. 8–9.

Fenton, M. and Hughes, P. (1989) *Passivity to Empowerment: A Living Skills Curriculum for People with Disabilities*. London: Royal Association for Disability and Rehabilitation (RADAR).

Hammond, M. and Collins, R. (1991) *Self-directed Learning: Critical Perspective*. London: Kogan Page.

Harries, W. (1990) 'Students with Severe Learning Difficulties and Social Integration', in Open University Diploma in Post Compulsory Education (Part B) *Offprint Book 6*, Milton Keynes: Open University Press.

Kjellen, G. (1991) 'The Kurator System in Denmark', in OECD, *Disabled Youth: From School to Work*, Paris: OECD.

Turnham, M. (1991) 'Supporting Special Needs in Further Education', in Booth, T., Swann, W., Masterton, M. and Potts, P. (eds) *Learning for All: Policies for Diversity in Education*. London: Routledge.

Unwin, L. (1990) 'The Competence Race: We Are All Qualified Now', in Corbett, J. (ed.) *Uneasy Transitions*. Lewes: Falmer Press.

Warnock, M. (1991) 'Equality Fifteen Years On', *Oxford Review of Education*, vol. 17, no. 2, pp. 145–54.

CONCLUSION

Ainley, P. (1991) *Young People Leaving Home*. London: Cassell.

Atkinson, D. and Williams, F. (1990) *Know Me As I Am*. London: Hodder and Stoughton.

Bishop, J., Gregory, S. and Sheldon, L. (1991) 'School and Beyond', in Taylor, G. and Bishop, J. (eds.) *Being Deaf*. London: Pinter Press.

Cooper, D. (1991) 'The Implications of the Contents of the White Paper for Young People and Adults with Special Needs and Staff who Work with Them', National Council for Special Education (NCSE) Conference, Grimsby, 23 November.

Daunt, P. (1991) *Meeting Disability: A European Response*. London: Cassell.

Doyle, P. (1988) *The God Squad*. London: Corgi.

Fulcher, G. (1989) *Disability Policies*. Lewes: Falmer Press.

McGinty, J. and Fish, J. (1992) *Learning Support for Young People in Transition: Leaving School for Further Education and Work*. Milton Keynes: Open University Press.

Morris, J. (1989) *Able Lives*. London: The Women's Press.

Morris, J. (1991) *Pride Against Prejudice*. London: The Women's Press.

Mottley, S. (1991) *Tough Cookie*. London: Hodder and Stoughton.

OECD (1991) *Disabled Youth: From School to Work*. Paris: OECD.

Wertheimer, A. (ed.) (1991) *Employment Opportunities for People with Severe Learning Difficulties*. London: King's Fund Centre.

INDEX

125